Joseph

# Joseph

*From Dreamer to Deliverer*

R.C. SPROUL

 LIGONIER MINISTRIES

*Joseph: From Dreamer to Deliverer*
© 2023 by the R.C. Sproul Trust

Published by Ligonier Ministries
421 Ligonier Court, Sanford, FL 32771
Ligonier.org

Printed in China
Amity Printing Company
0000324
First printing

ISBN 978-1-64289-547-6 (Hardcover)
ISBN 978-1-64289-548-3 (ePub)

Cover design: Ligonier Creative
Interior design and typeset: Katherine Lloyd, The DESK

Ligonier Ministries edited and adapted Dr. R.C. Sproul's original
material to create this volume. We are thankful to Mrs. Vesta Sproul
for her invaluable help on this project.

Library of Congress Control Number: 2023933392

# Contents

# 1

# The Dreamer

When we read the biblical accounts of the Old Testament patriarchs and prophets, we're accustomed to seeing their portraits, warts and all. The Bible doesn't hesitate to broadcast the sins of the saints. We read of the adultery and murder committed by King David and the deceitfulness of Abraham, but for one Old Testament saint, we must press very hard to find anything blameworthy in his character. That person is Joseph.

So extraordinary is Joseph's virtue that throughout church history, many interpreters have seen him as a type or forerunner of our Lord Himself. That view is not universally held, but it is understandable why such a view has been ventured, considering Joseph's sterling character.

We are told in Genesis about Joseph's mother, Rachel. His father, Jacob, had to work seven years for his father-in-law, Laban, before he could marry Rachel. Yet Laban deceived him, and after that seven-year period, Jacob was given Leah as his wife instead of Rachel. Jacob was permitted by Laban to marry Rachel just a week after he had married Leah—but only after he agreed to labor another seven years for Rachel. Joseph was the child of Jacob's old age and the firstborn to Rachel.

Genesis 37 picks up the narrative of Joseph's life:

Jacob lived in the land of his father's sojournings, in the land of Canaan. These are the generations of Jacob. Joseph, being seventeen years old, was pasturing the flock with his brothers. He was a boy with the sons of Bilhah and Zilpah, his father's wives. And Joseph brought a bad report of them to their father. (vv. 1–2)

Some have argued that at the very beginning of the Joseph narrative, we see a defect in his character. Here was a boy who was bringing a bad report about his brothers to their father—a report that would not be taken kindly by the brothers. If we read back into this text the whole character of Joseph manifested in his biographical sketch in Scripture, however, we are inclined to think that the report, though negative, was true and that Joseph could be excused for giving a higher response to a higher duty—namely, fidelity to his father over fidelity to his brothers.

This interpretation hints at a similar incident in the life of Jesus. We know next to nothing of Jesus' boyhood years, except for the occasion when He visited the temple in Jerusalem at age twelve. He stayed behind in the temple to talk with the teachers on matters of theology, and His parents were unaware that He had been left behind. Presumably, the men were traveling with the men, and the women with the women and children. Joseph probably thought Jesus was with Mary, and Mary thought He was with Joseph.

When they hurried back to Jerusalem and found their son disputing with the theologians in the temple, they rebuked Him. Jesus answered His parents, "Did you not know that I must be in my Father's house?" (Luke 2:49). Jesus' behavior was not sinful but righteous. He was obeying His Father. Joseph was likely acting in a similar manner when he gave his parents an honest report.

> Now Israel [Jacob] loved Joseph more than any other of his sons, because he was the son of his old age. And he made him a robe of many colors. But when his brothers saw that their father loved him more than all his brothers, they hated him and could not speak peacefully to him. (Gen. 37:3–4)

What follows is not only the story of a boy but a story that becomes foundational to the history of the nation of Israel. It is a history that takes a pivotal turn because of human envy and jealousy. Early in the narrative of Joseph, we are introduced to the salient point that for whatever reason, his brothers despised him. They would not even speak peaceably with him, meaning that their attitude toward him was one of belligerence. They were hostile toward him. Their hostility was rooted (at least initially) not so much in what Joseph did but in what Joseph's father did. They despised Joseph because of the special affection he received from their father.

Isn't it interesting how hostile the people of Israel were toward Jesus, who was the beloved of the Father? In the case of Joseph and his brothers, we have sibling rivalry. Any parent of more than one child must deal with the problem of sibling rivalries. They are common in the home. Unless you've been a parent, it's hard to know the struggle that parents can experience at times with showing favoritism to their own children.

Jacob loved Joseph more than he loved the rest of his sons. This doesn't mean that he didn't love the rest of his children, but he had a greater love for Joseph because Joseph was the firstborn to Rachel and the child of Jacob's old age. Jacob manifested this favoritism by giving Joseph a tunic of many colors. We take for granted the ability to go shopping and choose our garments from myriads of shades, and as a result, we forget that in the ancient world the producing of color in a garment was a laborious process and that colored garments were exceedingly expensive. Most of the clothing worn by the inhabitants of the ancient Near East was black, brown, or sometimes white, but not the rich colors and hues of the rainbow.

The tunic that Jacob gave to Joseph, however, not only had one color but had a variety of colors, making it all the more expensive and all the more treasured. This extraordinary gift singled Joseph out from the rest of the boys. It's hard to imagine a parent's doing that without knowing the contention that would arise from such an obvious sign of favoritism, but we can't fault Joseph. He was the recipient of the gift, not the giver.

When his brothers saw that their father loved Joseph more than he loved them, they hated Joseph, not their father, and they could not speak peaceably to him. To make matters worse, Joseph received a gift not only from his earthly father but from his heavenly Father. He was endowed with the ability to interpret dreams.

Now Joseph had a dream, and when he told it to his brothers they hated him even more. He said to them, "Hear this dream that I have dreamed: Behold, we were binding sheaves in the field, and behold, my sheaf arose and stood upright. And behold, your sheaves gathered around it and bowed down to my sheaf." His brothers said to him, "Are you indeed to reign over us? Or are you indeed to rule over us?" So they hated him even more for his dreams and for his words. (vv. 5–8)

It's one thing that God gave this dream to Joseph; it's another thing for Joseph to tell the dream to his brothers. We can only speculate about Joseph's motive. If we take a darker view, we can see Joseph as a seventeen-year-old who was sick of being hated by his brothers. He was tired of being treated unjustly because of his father's favor. So to get even with them, he recounted this wonderful dream in which he saw the sheaves of wheat bowing down before him.

The dream was prophetic, and it would be fulfilled to the very detail in the future. We must ask, though, why Joseph shared the content of this dream with his brothers. On one hand, it could be that he was motivated to gloat over his brothers and to glory in the favoritism of his father.

On the other hand, a more charitable judgment would say that Joseph could have been instructed by God to make the contents of this dream known. Normally when God reveals something in Scripture to one of His prophets, the purpose of that revelation is to make it known for the edification of others. That would be consistent with Joseph's explaining the content of the dream.

If we learn anything about Joseph through examining his life, it is that he was not stupid. He would have to assume that if his brothers hated him already, telling them this dream would only exacerbate the situation. But we cannot know for certain whether his relating of the dream was out of obedience to God or out of spite.

> Then he dreamed another dream and told it to his
> brothers and said, "Behold, I have dreamed another
> dream. Behold, the sun, the moon, and eleven stars

were bowing down to me." But when he told it to his father and to his brothers, his father rebuked him and said to him, "What is this dream that you have dreamed? Shall I and your mother and your brothers indeed come to bow ourselves to the ground before you?" And his brothers were jealous of him, but his father kept the saying in mind. (vv. 9–11)

At this point Jacob was angry and joined in the rebuke against Joseph because the second dream indicated that not only would Joseph's eleven brothers bow down before him but his parents would as well. This was more than Jacob could handle.

In Israel, it was the father, not the son, who was exalted in the family. For example, according to Jewish custom, when the father walked into a room, the sons had a duty to stand up as a display of respect to their father. The only exception to this rule was if the son became a rabbi. The office of rabbi was so honored among the Jewish people that the custom would be reversed. If a son who was a rabbi walked into the room, the father would rise out of honor to him.

Joseph, however, was a seventeen-year-old boy. He was not a rabbi. When he suggested that his father would bow down before him, Jacob rebuked him. Yet while the brothers' envy toward Joseph increased, Jacob meditated on what Joseph had spoken. Even though he was upset and rebuked Joseph, Jacob still did not definitively conclude that this was just a dream of Joseph's vain imagination; rather, he wondered whether it was from God.

2

# A Sin
# Concealed

After his first dream, Joseph announced to his brothers that at some point in the future they would bow down before him. He then had a second dream indicating that not only would his brothers bow down to him, but his parents would as well. Genesis 37:12 picks up the narrative:

> Now his brothers went to pasture their father's flock near Shechem. And Israel said to Joseph, "Are not your brothers pasturing the flock at Shechem? Come, I will send you to them." And he said to him,

"Here I am." So he said to him, "Go now, see if it is well with your brothers and with the flock, and bring me word." So he sent him from the Valley of Hebron, and he came to Shechem. (vv. 12–14)

You might get the impression that Jacob was merely sending Joseph down the road a bit—perhaps half a mile or so—to the fields where the brothers were tending the flock. Remember, however, that the Jewish people at this time were seminomads. They lived in tents and moved around as their livestock found fertile pastures in which to graze. Since the land was somewhat sparse in terms of grazing areas and given to seasonal fluctuations, they had to move around a lot.

In some cases, the seminomads would find a place to live and assign the task of caring for the sheep to their sons or their servants. The keepers of the flock followed the sheep into sometimes distant areas while the main family remained rooted in one place. Here, we are told that Jacob sent Joseph from the Valley of Hebron to Shechem, which was a distance of about forty miles. For a teenage boy living during this time, traveling alone was quite a journey. There was no train to ride, and he would risk encountering bandits and other dangers. We can see why Jacob would be interested in hearing from his sons. Since they were so far away, Jacob couldn't receive regular updates from them. By sending Joseph, Jacob could obtain a report regarding the brothers and the flock.

Joseph set out, and "a man found him wandering in the fields. And the man asked him, 'What are you seeking?'" (v. 15). Presumably, Joseph had made it to Shechem. He was wandering around in the fields, looking for his brothers and for his father's flocks, and he hadn't been able to find them. This man found Joseph and asked him what he was seeking. "'I am seeking my brothers,' he said. 'Tell me, please, where they are pasturing the flock.' And the man said, 'They have gone away, for I heard them say, "Let us go to Dothan."' So Joseph went after his brothers and found them at Dothan" (vv. 16–17).

Dothan is about ten miles farther north of the Valley of Hebron, so Joseph traveled more than fifty miles to find his brothers and the flock. In verse 18 we read,

"They saw him from afar, and before he came near to them they conspired against him to kill him." Even though they had been removed from their brother, the raging jealousy had built up to such a degree that now they were conspiring with one another on how to kill Joseph.

> They said to one another, "Here comes this dreamer. Come now, let us kill him and throw him into one of the pits. Then we will say that a fierce animal has devoured him, and we will see what will become of his dreams. But when Reuben heard it, he rescued him out of their hands, saying, "Let us not take his life." And Reuben said to them, "Shed no blood; throw him into this pit here in the wilderness, but do not lay a hand on him"—that he might rescue him out of their hand to restore him to his father. So when Joseph came to his brothers, they stripped him of his robe, the robe of many colors that he wore. And they took him and threw him into a pit. The pit was empty; there was no water in it. (vv. 19–24)

The hostility that had taken root in his brothers' hearts was profound at this point. Yet Reuben interceded on behalf of Joseph, and he came up with a counterscheme. He thought he could satisfy the brothers' vengeful rage by deserting Joseph in the pit, and then later he could sneak back and rescue Joseph.

It's significant that there was no water in the pit. In the desert region of the ancient Near East, there was very sparse growth on which to graze livestock. It was necessary in those days, as it is today, for shepherds working in the heat to carry an abundance of water with them. Wells were extremely important in Jacob's day. To throw a young man into a pit that is exposed to the beating sun and not provide him with any water is to guarantee his certain death.

"Then they sat down to eat" (v. 25). This speaks volumes about the hardness of heart of Joseph's brothers that they could throw him into a pit, exposing him to certain death, and then sit down and devour a meal. Many people find that whenever they feel guilty, they feel it in their stomachs. There's nothing worse than the upset stomach that comes from feeling awful about one's sin. That didn't bother these men, however. They sat down and gorged themselves with a meal.

> And looking up they saw a caravan of Ishmaelites coming from Gilead, with their camels bearing gum, balm, and myrrh, on their way to carry it down to Egypt. Then Judah said to his brothers, "What profit is it if we kill our brother and conceal his blood? Come, let us sell him to the Ishmaelites, and let not our hand be upon him, for he is our brother, our own flesh." And his brothers listened to him. (vv. 25–27)

Caravans were used to transport merchants' goods to various commercial centers. This particular caravan was laden with precious spices and ointments being taken from the northern regions down to Egypt, where there was a lucrative market for these goods.

We would expect Reuben and Judah, two of the elder brothers, to have a little more wisdom and a little more sense of protective care for their younger brother.

Now both have interceded against the conspiracy to kill Joseph.

When Judah made his suggestion, he apparently did not know of Reuben's secret plan to rescue Joseph after the brothers left him in the pit. So Judah came up with his own plan for how to persuade the brothers not to kill Joseph. It's hardly as compassionate as Reuben's plan, though. We don't know for certain whether Judah was acting out of concern for Joseph or whether he was only aggravating the plot by seeking to find some profit in it. Either way, he explained his plan as a better one. Instead of killing Joseph, they could get rid of him just as easily by selling him to the Ishmaelites, and they'd make a profit as well. They'd be rid of Joseph, and his blood wouldn't be on their hands.

> Then Midianite traders passed by. And they drew Joseph up and lifted him out of the pit, and sold him to the Ishmaelites for twenty shekels of silver. They took Joseph to Egypt. When Reuben returned to the pit and saw that Joseph was not in the pit, he tore his

clothes and returned to his brothers and said, "The boy is gone, and I, where shall I go?" (vv. 28–30)

Many commentators in church history have seen in Joseph an Old Testament type of Christ, and here we see another reason for that typological interpretation. Joseph was betrayed and sold into slavery for twenty pieces of silver, just as Jesus was betrayed by one of His "brothers," as it were, His disciple, into the hands of His enemies for thirty pieces of silver.

Apparently, Reuben had been absent during the brothers' further discussion and change of plans, so his plan to rescue Joseph from the pit went awry.

Then they took Joseph's robe and slaughtered a goat and dipped the robe in the blood. And they sent the robe of many colors and brought it to their father and said, "This we have found; please identify whether it is your son's robe or not." And he [Jacob] identified it and said, "It is my son's robe. A fierce animal has devoured him. Joseph is without doubt torn to pieces." Then Jacob tore his garments and put sackcloth on his loins and mourned for his son many days. All his sons and all his daughters rose up to comfort him, but he refused to be comforted and said, "No, I shall go down to Sheol to my son, mourning." Thus his father wept for him. (vv. 31–35)

The brothers displayed remarkable hypocrisy on this occasion. They are the ones who had stripped Joseph of his coat, dipped it in the blood of a goat, and presented the tunic that they knew very well was Joseph's. They could hardly mistake this coat, for it was extraordinary and unique in the first place. If somebody tried this scheme today, it wouldn't take long for the police to see that the blood on the garment was not human blood. In antiquity, however, no blood analysis or DNA testing was available to implicate the brothers in their crime.

Jacob reacted to the evidence in front of him, and that evidence proved to him beyond a reasonable doubt that his son had been killed by an animal. It's striking that Jacob was tortured by grief—a grief that had to be mixed with a sense of guilt. Most of his grief was over the death of his beloved son, but mixed with that grief was the knowledge that it had been his own idea to send his young son on this arduous journey and to put his life at risk.

While we must be careful not to overdo the typological references from Joseph to Jesus, we do see a connection between the two, in that Jesus was put to death because He was sent on a mission by His Father. We must not include in this comparison a heresy called Patripassianism, which teaches that the Father suffered in the death of the Son on the cross. Certainly in the human relationship between Jacob and Joseph, the father suffered enormously in his perception of the loss of the son.

While Jacob was beside himself with grief and would not stop mourning, his other sons and daughters sought to comfort him. It is egregious that all the passion of Jacob was not enough to move the brothers to repentance. They saw the consequences of their crime in the pain of their own father every day. They sinned not only against their brother but against their father as well, and they compounded that sin by hypocritically making a show of bringing comfort to their father.

Notice that Jacob said, "I shall go down to Sheol to my son, mourning" (v. 35). One of the techniques used by novelists in general and by mystery writers in particular is foreshadowing. The author sets up a sequence and alerts the reader to a danger that's about to take place. In this case, the foreshadowing is Jacob's prediction regarding himself. He said that there wouldn't be any end to his grief—that he would go to his own grave and join Joseph in the grave, grieving. Because we know the outcome of the story, we know that Jacob's conclusion is wrong, but it adds to the drama. At this point, Jacob had no hope for the future.

Crime begets crime. Few of us have been guilty of killing a brother or a sister, but all of us have been guilty of sin. When we commit sin, we do several things, one of which is to try to justify our sin to ourselves, to rationalize it, to make it seem that our sin was the right thing to do at the time. Oftentimes, after we attempt to justify our sin, we then try to conceal it. We see that these men went to great lengths to conceal their sin. Not only did they try to conceal it in the first instance, but one lie led to another lie and another lie and another lie. This is the human pattern. It's the way we sin. Instead of standing in total judgment of these men, let us be careful to learn from their pattern, lest we continue to duplicate it.

3

# A Strange Vocation

After the brothers conspired to do away with Joseph, settling on a plan to sell him to a caravan of merchants traveling south toward Egypt, Genesis 37 ends with this footnote: "Meanwhile the Midianites had sold him in Egypt to Potiphar, an officer of Pharaoh, the captain of the guard" (v. 36).

At this point, there is a sudden intrusion into this narrative of Joseph's life. Genesis 38 diverts the narrative from the story of Joseph to the scandalous story of Judah and Tamar. Consequently, we should step back and ask why Moses, the author of Genesis, interrupted the Joseph narrative with this story.

The story of Judah and Tamar exhibits a pattern that we see repeated throughout the early chapters of Genesis: that of the existence of a godly line of descendants and a wicked line of descendants and the consequences when those lines mix. After the fall, the first homicide occurred as Cain killed Abel, after which Cain's descendants multiplied evil. On the other hand, Seth, the son born to Adam and Eve to replace Abel, begat a line of godly descendants.

There are thus two lines in the early chapters of Genesis: one following the pattern of Cain in wickedness and the other following the line of Seth in godliness ("the sons of God," Gen. 6:2). Yet the two lines intermarried, and when that happened, God saw that man's wickedness was great and that the world was filled with evil. God then decided to destroy all humanity except for one family that would be preserved as the root, or the remnant, out of which redemption would come, and it was the family of Noah.

We see the lines mixing again in chapter 38. Jacob

was an heir to the covenant of Abraham. He was part of that group of people who were separated from the world. Yet his son Judah intermarried with a pagan (v. 2). Because of this, the family structure of Jacob started to fall apart as his sons committed wickedness (vv. 6–10).

Jacob's family was in Canaan, and they were already becoming unholy. They needed to be separated from Canaan and placed in a distinctive environment. This will occur later in the story when Jacob's family goes down to Egypt and takes up residence in the land of Goshen (chs. 45–47). The story of Judah and Tamar in chapter 38 points to the consequences of the mixing between the godly and wicked lines and the need for God's people to be separate, set apart unto Him.

After Joseph was sold to the Midianite traders, the Midianites took him to Egypt and sold him. In the providence of God, a caravan passed by at just that moment. The caravan happened to be traveling south rather than north—on their way to Egypt, not from Egypt. Because of the direction in which the caravan was headed, the Israelites eventually ended up in Egypt and in bondage.

We are told at the end of chapter 37 that the Midianites turned around and sold Joseph to Potiphar, a man of great importance, wealth, and status in the Egyptian government. Potiphar oversaw the palace guard of Pharaoh. The Joseph narrative picks up again in chapter 39:

> Now Joseph had been brought down to Egypt, and Potiphar, an officer of Pharaoh, the captain of the guard, an Egyptian, had bought him from the Ishmaelites who had brought him down there. The LORD was with Joseph, and he became a successful man, and he was in the house of his Egyptian master. (vv. 1–2)

Joseph was removed not only from his family and his homeland but also from the presence of the worship of Yahweh. He was transported to a foreign country. Yet even though his family wasn't with him, the Lord was with him, even in the pagan land of Egypt. We are also told that Joseph was a successful man. He was gifted by God and was an exceptional administrator and manager. As a result, he was put in a position of management in the house of this high-ranking official of Egypt.

Joseph was not relegated to the role of galley slave or field worker in Egypt. He was put to work in a responsible position, and he obviously manifested skill and ability. Joseph's vocation at this point in life was, to all outward appearances, a secular vocation. The word *vocation* comes from the Latin word that means "to call," so a vocation is a calling. A vocation need not be a call to ordained ministry. One of the important insights of the Reformation was that every believer has a vocation and that God calls men and women to tasks that are not always overtly religious. Joseph's vocation was of crucial importance to the work of the kingdom of God, but his vocation was worked out in the secular arena of political administration.

The gift of administration is an underappreciated spiritual gift (see 1 Cor. 12:28). Every organization— the church, a business, a sports team—has to be managed so that it allocates its resources in a productive way. The people who have those administrative gifts are extremely important for the well-being of the enterprise. In the Christian community, we tend to act as though the only viable religious activity consists of those who are involved in preaching, teaching, evangelism, and so on, and we forget that none of that can be done—or at least be done prudently and effectively—without someone's administering it.

Joseph was God's anointed man in Egypt. In a real sense, he was the advance man whom God sent down to Egypt to prepare the way for the migration of his entire family. He was working as a slave, but God was with him. He was exercising his gifts in obedience to his master who owned him, yet at the same time, he was fulfilling his destiny under the providence of God. So God was with Joseph, and Joseph prospered—or at least Potiphar prospered because of Joseph.

> His master saw that the LORD was with him and that the LORD caused all that he did to succeed in his hands. So Joseph found favor in his sight and attended him, and he made him overseer of his house and put him in charge of all that he had.

From the time that he made him overseer in his house and over all that he had, the LORD blessed the Egyptian's house for Joseph's sake; the blessing of the LORD was on all that he had, in house and field. So he left all that he had in Joseph's charge, and because of him he had no concern about anything but the food he ate. (vv. 3–6)

Potiphar saw that this was a good situation. He was aware of Joseph's gifts, and he became convinced that the God of the Hebrews was with Joseph. Everything that Joseph put his hand to prospered. Potiphar reaped the benefit, which becomes significant when Joseph later runs into problems in Potiphar's house, problems that could have ended in his execution.

At this point, however, Potiphar was pleased because his servant Joseph was making all his affairs prosper. He continued to increase Joseph's responsibilities, first making him overseer of his house, and then putting everything that he had under Joseph's management.

We might think that things were starting to look up for Joseph as we reach this point in the narrative of his life. Perhaps Joseph thought so too. Yet as we will see multiple times, just as things seem to be trending upward, another heart-wrenching setback is about to come.

# 4

# Seduction Resisted

Joseph seems to get into one predicament after another, and each is worse than the one that precedes it. We saw the first problem when he was sold into slavery by his brothers. That seemed to turn out all right when the slave master who purchased him promoted him to a position of importance, one in which Joseph was given absolute trust in Potiphar's household.

Then things took another turn for the worse, and we will see this pattern repeated throughout Joseph's story. Genesis 39:6 gives us another foreboding hint of what is to come by providing a seemingly innocuous physical description of Joseph: "Now Joseph was handsome in form and appearance." Though the description of Joseph is positive, it's not included in the narrative without reason, implying that something bad is about to take place.

"And after a time his master's wife cast her eyes on Joseph and said, 'Lie with me'" (v. 7). This is one of the most destructive attempts at seduction that we see in Scripture, surpassed only by the serpent's seducing of Adam and Eve and by Satan's attempt to seduce Jesus. Again, we see a parallel between Joseph and Jesus in that Joseph was the target of seduction. We will also see that, like Jesus, Joseph resisted the attempt and remained virtuous and chaste.

Let's consider this scenario. Joseph is a young man who is being targeted for seduction by an experienced woman. He is a single man, a lonely man, who has been forsaken by his family and is living in a far country. Remember the prodigal son, whose licentious lifestyle began when he left the moral restraints of his family and community and ventured into a far country where he was anonymous. As this temptation unfolds, Joseph resides in a land that does not share the values and laws that are sacred to the people of Israel.

Yet we remember the statement "The LORD was with Joseph" (Gen. 39:2). If ever a young man was vulnerable to temptation, it was Joseph. What restrained him? A few things are obvious: (1) the grace of God and the presence of God; (2) Joseph's commitment and loyalty to his earthly master, this woman's husband; and (3) Joseph's own personal integrity.

Joseph knew that this temptation came from a woman who held enormous power over him. She was the mistress of the house, and she was obviously not afraid to use the power she possessed.

> But he refused and said to his master's wife, "Behold, because of me my master has no concern about anything in the house, and he has put everything that he has in my charge. He is not greater in this house than I am, nor has he kept back anything from me except you, because you are his wife." (vv. 8–9)

Joseph refused the seductive invitation. He said to her: "Don't you realize that your husband has given me authority over everything in this house? He's given me a high degree of freedom. He's put only one restriction on me, and it's you. And you are asking me to violate the one area that is off-limits to me."

A similar situation occurred earlier in the book of Genesis. "You may surely eat of every tree of the garden, but of the tree of the knowledge of good and evil you shall not eat, for in the day that you eat of it you shall surely die" (2:16–17). God gave Adam and Eve freedom in the highest magnitude with only one restriction. One tree in the garden was off-limits to them, and that tree became the focal point of satanic seduction. The same thing was happening here to Joseph.

Joseph's first response was that he could not do such a thing and violate Potiphar. Yet he didn't stop there. "How then can I do this great wickedness and sin against God?" (39:9). He was not only saying, "I won't"; he was saying, "I can't." Many people in today's culture, even those who profess Christianity, are involved in illicit sexual activity because they have completely thrown away the moral restraints of Scripture. Joseph, however, understood the law of God, so what restrained him was his devotion to God.

"And as she spoke to Joseph day after day, he would not listen to her, to lie beside her or to be with her" (v. 10). This was not a one-time temptation. This woman was relentless. Day after day, she kept coming to Joseph, trying to find his moral weakness, trying to get him to surrender to her, trying to get him to compromise. Such pursuit, with a woman initiating the seduction, could be tremendously flattering to the male ego. That makes Joseph's vulnerability all the greater.

This reminds us of Satan's tempting Jesus in the wilderness. We are told in Scripture that even after Jesus overcame the temptation experience and Satan left Him for a season, Satan wasn't yet through with Him. Similarly, Potiphar's wife didn't know how to quit. She kept it up, and Joseph tried to avoid her.

> But one day, when he went into the house to do
> his work and none of the men of the house was
> there in the house, she caught him by his garment,

saying, "Lie with me." But he left his garment in her hand and fled and got out of the house. And as soon as she saw that he had left his garment in her hand and had fled out of the house, she called to the men of her household and said to them, "See, he has brought among us a Hebrew to laugh at us. He came in to me to lie with me, and I cried out with a loud voice." (vv. 11–14)

Once again, Joseph was at the center of a crime that involved circumstantial evidence. The first had been when his brothers presented the evidence of a tunic drenched in blood to cover up their crime of selling Joseph into slavery. In Potiphar's house, Joseph was put into a situation in which Potiphar's wife attempted the seduction again when nobody else was there.

He fled, leaving behind the garment that she had grabbed hold of. He left physical evidence that would be used against him when she falsely charged him with attempted rape. Only the eyes of God were there, and God knew the innocence of His servant Joseph.

Yet what happened to him because of his virtue was calamitous.

There is a clear contrast between this situation with Joseph and David's life. David was a man after God's own heart, a friend of God. He was righteous and devout. Yet when he saw Bathsheba bathing, he was overcome with lust. He set aside all his ethics, his commitment to God's law, and plunged into horrific sin that was destructive for him and for all Israel. Joseph, by contrast, remained steadfast in his virtue day after day in the face of relentless pursuit by Potiphar's wife.

There is a saying in our culture: "Hell hath no fury like a woman scorned." The fury of hell would soon fall on Joseph.

# 5

# True Success

Joseph found himself in a terrible predicament when Potiphar's wife relentlessly tried to seduce him. And yet he resisted her because he refused to commit such great wickedness against God. In her desperation, she grabbed him, and when Joseph fled from her presence, his garment was left behind in her hand. How did Potiphar's wife respond?

> And as soon as she saw that he had left his garment in her hand and had fled out of the house, she called to the men of her household and said

to them, "See, he has brought among us a Hebrew to laugh at us. He came in to me to lie with me, and I cried out with a loud voice. And as soon as he heard that I lifted up my voice and cried out, he left his garment beside me and fled and got out of the house." (Gen. 39:13–15)

The woman's vanity was crushed by Joseph's rejection, so she accused him of attempted rape. She made clear that the man whom she was accusing was not an Egyptian, almost as if to say: "He's not one of us. Who are you going to believe, me or him?"

Then she laid up his garment by her until his master came home, and she told him the same story, saying, "The Hebrew servant, whom you have brought among us, came in to me to laugh at me. But as soon as I lifted up my voice and cried, he left his garment beside me and fled out of the house."

As soon as his master heard the words that his wife spoke to him, "This is the way your servant treated me," his anger was kindled. And Joseph's master took him and put him into the prison, the place where the king's prisoners were confined, and he was there in prison. (vv. 16–20)

The fact that Potiphar's anger was aroused indicates that he believed these false charges. After all, she had the evidence. It's understandable why he would have been angered. His wife had been violated, and violated by a slave—and not just any slave. She had been violated by a slave to whom Potiphar had granted special privileges and favors.

So then, why didn't Potiphar have Joseph immediately executed? Perhaps it was because he knew his wife, but he also knew Joseph. He knew Joseph's character. Joseph seems to have thus gotten off somewhat easy, which hints that Potiphar may have harbored doubts about his wife's accusation.

So God seems to have rewarded Joseph for his obedience by having him thrown into prison. We may conclude from this story that righteousness does not pay. Joseph may have thought to himself that he would have been better off succumbing to the temptation, for

JOSEPH

then he may have still enjoyed the status that he had in Potiphar's house. Instead, he was in prison. Yet we see from Joseph's conduct and character in prison that there was no expression of hostility toward God for his circumstances.

In this, Joseph was like the Apostle Paul, who was no stranger to the jail system of his day. Paul spent a lot of time in prison, and every time he was there, it was on false charges. The Apostle said of his own life: "For I have learned in whatever situation I am to be content. I know how to be brought low, and I know how to abound" (Phil. 4:11–12).

That's what we find in the character of Joseph. We read this after Potiphar put Joseph into prison: "But the Lord was with Joseph" (Gen. 39:21). That's the second time we read this statement. The first was after Joseph had been sold into slavery and brought to Egypt (39:2).

Joseph's situation took a turn for the worse. He was thrown into prison, where his abandonment seemed to be complete and his solitude absolute—except that the Lord was with him. We see in this story not simply Joseph's fidelity amid these difficult circumstances;

we see also the fidelity of God. God promised that He would be with this man, and He did not depart from him. Whether in slavery or in prison, God was there.

This is an important point for us to remember. Prosperity preachers today tell us that if we're Christians, we will never suffer. Even a cursory reading of the Scriptures reveals that this is a lie, and we should not be deceived by it. God does not promise us freedom from pain, persecution, tribulation, or suffering. On the contrary, He promises that these things will happen to us, but in the midst of these circumstances, He also promises His presence. We see this demonstrated in Joseph's life.

"The LORD was with Joseph and showed him steadfast love" (v. 21). It certainly doesn't seem as though Joseph was getting much steadfast love. He was certainly not getting any justice. "And [God] gave him favor in the sight of the keeper of the prison" (v. 21). When Joseph had been sold into slavery, God blessed him, in that he won the favor of Potiphar.

Every time Joseph was shown favoritism, he got into trouble. He had received great favor from his father, Jacob. He had received Potiphar's favor. Now the warden of the prison looked kindly upon Joseph. We may wonder what it was about this young man that people were so favorably disposed toward him. It was probably a matter not simply of Joseph's personality and character but also of his skills. Even in prison, he began to use the gifts that God had given him in leadership, management, and administration.

> And the keeper of the prison put Joseph in charge of all the prisoners who were in the prison. Whatever was done there, he was the one who did it. The keeper of the prison paid no attention to anything that was in Joseph's charge, because the LORD was with him. And whatever he did, the LORD made it succeed. (vv. 22–23)

While Joseph was in Potiphar's household, Potiphar had delegated authority over his entire household to Joseph. And now the warden placed Joseph in charge of the whole prison. The text exactly repeats what had been said of Joseph when he began to manage

Potiphar's affairs. He managed things so superbly that the person to whom Joseph was answerable stopped bothering to supervise him. Nobody was looking over his shoulder. Everything that he did prospered. He was better at the job than the warden was.

Wherever Joseph was, he did his work to the glory of God. No job was too menial or too low for him to apply his energy in this way. This was very likely because of his relationship with God.

The Scriptures tell us again: "The LORD was with [Joseph]. And whatever he did, the LORD made it succeed" (v. 23). Joseph was in prison by the providence of God, and the success that he found in prison was not simply the result of his own ability or energy. It was the Lord who made him prosper. He understood that he was to do everything in his power to the glory of God but that God would ultimately bring the increase and the prosperity.

Psalm 23:6 says, "Surely goodness and mercy shall follow me all the days of my life." In Hebrew, the verb translated as "follow" means "to pursue" or "to chase after." That is what we see in the life of Joseph. God's mercy followed him wherever he went; it chased him. He couldn't outrun the mercy and goodness of God. That's what it means to submit to the providence of God. Wherever we are, we can know not only that He is there but that He is pursuing us with His mercy and with His goodness.

# 6

# The Meaning
# of Dreams

Joseph prospered during his time in prison. Just as he had impressed Potiphar and had been placed over Potiphar's household, Joseph impressed the keeper of the prison and soon rose to the level of a highly trusted inmate. As a result, the warden set Joseph over the rest of the prisoners. We pick up the next episode in Joseph's life here:

> Some time after this, the cupbearer of the king of Egypt and his baker committed an offense against their lord the king of Egypt. And Pharaoh was

angry with his two officers, the chief cupbearer and the chief baker, and he put them in custody in the house of the captain of the guard, in the prison where Joseph was confined. The captain of the guard appointed Joseph to be with them, and he attended them. They continued for some time in custody. (Gen. 40:1–4)

The Bible doesn't tell us exactly what offenses the cupbearer and the baker committed. We know only that whatever they did was so offensive to Pharaoh that he had them thrown in prison. Some have speculated that the royal prison held those who were accused of treason and that those confined there could reasonably expect to be executed at some point.

In the ancient world, it was not uncommon for political appointees to oversee various forms of a nation's industry. These people would serve in a type of "king's cabinet." For example, the chief baker would be responsible for overseeing the production of grain throughout the land. He wasn't simply the cook in the royal palace; rather, he had a high-ranking political position. Likewise, the cupbearer to the king was also the chief steward of the agriculture and foodstuffs for the entire nation. At least, that's the speculation.

To view this situation from our modern context, it would be akin to our president's sending the secretary of commerce and the secretary of agriculture to federal prison. In terms of why the cupbearer and the baker were imprisoned, however, we can only speculate. The Bible merely says that these men had offended Pharaoh. In any case, the captain of the guard charged Joseph with their oversight, so Joseph was responsible for these prisoners.

> And one night they both dreamed—the cupbearer and the baker of the king of Egypt, who were confined in the prison—each his own dream, and each dream with its own interpretation. When Joseph came to them in the morning, he saw that they were troubled. (vv. 5–6)

We are told that each of these men, on the same night, had a strange dream. This recalls the beginning of Joseph's narrative, when his interpretation of dreams led to his being sold into slavery by his brothers. In that case, the dreams that he had interpreted were his own.

The very thing that had gotten Joseph into trouble in the first place—the interpreting of dreams—was the occasion for his involvement in the royal court. When he came to their cells, Joseph noticed that the countenances of the cupbearer and baker were downcast. They were troubled in spirit.

> So he asked Pharaoh's officers who were with him in custody in his master's house, "Why are your faces downcast today?" They said to him, "We have had dreams, and there is no one to interpret them." And Joseph said to them, "Do not interpretations belong to God? Please tell them to me." (vv. 7–8)

Notice what Joseph said after he heard that they had had troublesome dreams. Much superstition abounded in that day regarding the meaning and interpretation of dreams. That's why every ancient court had a group of magicians, diviners, soothsayers, and fortunetellers who were believed to possess special insight into such things. Joseph said initially that God has the power to interpret dreams.

In a sense, Joseph was rebuking in advance those who would seek either to interpret their own dreams or to pursue pagan methods of interpreting their dreams. Throughout the Old Testament and even into the New Testament, one of the ways that God communicated to His people was through dreams. How did Joseph, the earthly father of Jesus, come to a state of peace in his soul about his betrothed, Mary, when she announced to him that she was with child? Joseph was upset when he heard Mary's news, and he planned "to divorce her quietly" (Matt. 1:19)—that is, until God revealed to him in a dream the truth about Mary's pregnancy. God spoke to him again later in a dream, warning him to flee from the wrath of Herod and to take Mary and the baby Jesus to Egypt.

At the same time, we see a misuse of dreams even in the Scriptures themselves. We recall Jeremiah's complaint when God spoke to him and revealed the impending judgment on Jerusalem. Yet every time Jeremiah warned about the destruction of Jerusalem, the false prophets rushed in and told their dreams to the people, saying that God had promised that they could be at ease in Zion, that there would never be any destruction of the Holy City. Jeremiah protested before God that he was in derision daily and that no one listened to him. Everything he taught was being condemned by these other prophets.

How did God respond? "Let the prophet who has a dream tell the dream, but let him who has my word speak my word faithfully" (Jer. 23:28). In the Bible, dreams were used as a means of divine revelation. Yet not every dream that a person had was divine revelation. The false prophets—who did not have the gift of interpreting dreams, who were not agents of revelation, who were not miraculously endowed by God to give this kind of interpretation—spoke falsehoods out of their dreams.

There was the true prophet, and there was the false prophet. The true prophet received the word of God. When the true prophet had a dream, God granted the interpretation of that dream because God was revealing Himself and His purposes through the dream. The false prophet, however, took whatever dreams he had, whether they were created by indigestion or his own fleshly desires, and acted as though they were the truth of God.

Unfortunately, false prophets are not confined to distant biblical history. They still exist today. This is why we must be extremely careful when people claim some kind of special, secret knowledge that they received while they were sleeping. Everything must be tested by the Word of God.

Joseph understood that principle, and so he said to these men that the interpretation of dreams belongs to God. When Joseph asked them, "Please tell them to me" (Gen. 40:8), he was saying a mouthful. He was saying that he could interpret the dreams because God had given him this gift. Joseph was claiming to be anointed by God with insight not from his own flesh, not from his own wisdom, but by virtue of the divine gift.

We may wonder how Joseph could be so confident after spending so much time in exile from his family and homeland, living in a foreign nation precisely because of former dreams he'd interpreted. We may think that after all the suffering and torment he had endured, he'd probably be scratching his head and thinking, "The last thing I'm ever going to do again is to trust a dream or presume to interpret a dream, because look what happened the last time I did that." Joseph didn't do that. Instead, he asked the two prisoners to tell him their dreams.

> So the chief cupbearer told his dream to Joseph and said to him, "In my dream there was a vine before me, and on the vine there were three branches. As soon as it budded, its blossoms shot forth, and the clusters ripened into grapes. Pharaoh's cup was in my hand, and I took the grapes and pressed them into Pharaoh's cup and placed the cup in Pharaoh's hand." (vv. 9–11)

This was a significant dream that impressed itself mightily on the dreamer. We've all experienced nightmares, possibly being awakened in terror at times. We go back to sleep, and in the morning we have a vague recollection that we had a dream, but for the life of us we can't remember the details. They seem to slip from our memory so quickly. By contrast, these men each had their dream only once, yet they could recite to Joseph every detail the next day.

Of course, the cupbearer was puzzled by his dream. Joseph said to him:

"This is its interpretation: the three branches are three days. In three days Pharaoh will lift up your head and restore you to your office, and you shall place Pharaoh's cup in his hand as formerly, when you were his cupbearer. Only remember me, when it is well with you, and please do me the kindness to mention me to Pharaoh, and so get me out of this house. For I was indeed stolen out of the land of the Hebrews, and here also I have done nothing that they should put me into the pit." (vv. 12–15)

This last statement that Joseph made, asking the cupbearer to remember him, is so important to our understanding of Joseph and of Scripture that we're going to delve into it more deeply in the next chapter.

55

For now, we'll simply note that Joseph gave the interpretation of the dream. The three branches indicated a period of three days, after which time Pharaoh would lift up the cupbearer's head. In other words, Pharaoh would exalt the cupbearer and restore him. The cupbearer would be brought back to the royal court, would be reinstated to his position, and would once again enjoy Pharaoh's good favor.

# 7

# Of God and Men

When Joseph gave the interpretation of the cup-bearer's dream, he made this one request:

"Only remember me, when it is well with you, and please do me the kindness to mention me to Pharaoh, and so get me out of this house. For I was indeed stolen out of the land of the Hebrews, and here also I have done nothing that they should put me into the pit." (Gen. 40:14–15)

Joseph, who had rested in the sovereignty of God and exhibited patience in his torment and loneliness for eleven years, was now asking for help.

The first thing to notice is that he was not praying to God to get him out of jail; he was pleading with the cupbearer to get him out of jail. He was asking the cupbearer to do him a favor. Some people might look at this and see it as a chink in Joseph's moral armor, supposing that he had suddenly lost faith and patience in divine sovereignty and was taking steps in the flesh to secure his own release. While it's true that we should always trust our lives and our futures to the hands of God, we are called to do our due diligence and be responsible stewards of what God has given us. There's nothing sinful or weak about Joseph's asking for help.

The second thing to notice is Joseph's plea: "For I was indeed stolen out of the land of the Hebrews, and here also I have done nothing that they should put me into the pit" (v. 15). Joseph said to the cupbearer: "I'm an innocent man. I'm in this prison for no good reason. Will you help plead my case? I've been falsely accused. I've done nothing wrong."

Jonathan Edwards discussed how love responds patiently to false charges and accusations. He raised a couple of questions: How are Christians to respond to slander or false charges made against them? How are Christians to guard their reputations?

Edwards went to great lengths to call Christians to a patient enduring of false accusations. In essence, he said that we should be willing to participate in the humiliation and suffering of Christ, who was constantly maligned and slandered and who spent His entire ministry being the victim of false charges. Jesus did not try to be vindicated from these charges. Instead, He returned good for evil, and as the Apostle says in Philippians 2, He "made Himself of no reputation" (v. 7, NKJV).

Edwards expounded Philippians 2 by saying that our Lord was willing to have a bad reputation, to have His name besmirched by false charges and vicious rumors. That is no small thing. We are very jealous as human beings to guard our reputations. We want people to think well of us. We daily seek the applause of people. Jesus, however, was willing to lay all that aside and become vilified. Edwards said that if we become vilified, we must remember that the enemies of the kingdom of God and our personal enemies cannot really harm us in any ultimate way.

In his hymn "A Mighty Fortress Is Our God," Martin Luther wrote: "Let goods and kindred go, this mortal life also; the body they may kill: God's truth abideth still." Luther suffered the loss of goods, the loss of physical pleasure, the loss of his reputation, and the loss of friends. He said that we should be willing to let all these things go for the sake of fidelity to the kingdom of God. That's Edwards' point as well.

Edwards essentially said: "What can they do to us? They can kill us; they can put us into prison; they can take away our reputations. But they can't get at the soul. They can't strip us of our salvation. That which is of enduring value can never be reached by the assaults of the enemy. The eternal values of life are safe in the hands of God." So Edwards said that we should not worry if they take away our goods, our bodies, or our reputations.

When Luther dealt with Philippians 2, his response seems to be opposite from Edwards'—at least at first glance. Specifically, Luther said that Christians should be very careful to guard their reputations, so much so that when they are falsely accused, they should plead innocence, lest by an undefended slander their reputations—and by extension, the reputation of the church and of Christ—are injured.

Luther was not saying that we should constantly seek vindication. He was saying that if we are falsely accused of something, we ought not to necessarily and at all times be silent, because in every culture when a person is accused of a crime and remains silent, the assumption that people make is that silence means guilt.

Luther gave a host of examples in Scripture in which biblical heroes who were falsely accused of crimes or sins stated their innocence, not the least of which was the Apostle Paul, who frequently in his letters responded to critics who were making false charges against him. Jesus Himself, when He was charged with sins, said: "Which one of you convicts me of sin? If I tell the truth, why do you not believe me?" (John 8:46). He humbly accepted the slander, and He was willing to suffer for the sake of the kingdom of God.

When asked, He spoke the truth and said that He was not guilty.

In interpreting this text, we have to walk a thin line between self-justification, in responding to every complaint or criticism that people level against us, and speaking the truth when it's a serious matter. As Christians, we should be able to absorb a lot of misrepresentation. Yet we also must do so with prudence and wisdom, defending ourselves not simply for the sake of defending ourselves but for the sake of defending the truth.

Joseph at this point in the narrative was pleading his case and asserting his innocence to the cupbearer. After Joseph interpreted the cupbearer's dream, the baker came forward:

> When the chief baker saw that the interpretation was favorable, he said to Joseph, "I also had a dream: there were three cake baskets on my head, and in the uppermost basket there were all sorts of baked food for Pharaoh, but the birds were eating it out of the basket on my head." And Joseph

answered and said, "This is its interpretation: the three baskets are three days." (Gen. 40:16–18)

The baker must have been thrilled. So far, this was the same thing that Joseph had said to the cupbearer: the three branches were three days, and the three baskets were three days. The baker probably couldn't wait to hear the rest of the interpretation.

"In three days Pharaoh will lift up your head— from you!—and hang you on a tree. And the birds will eat the flesh from you." (v. 19)

This was not what the baker was expecting to hear.

One thing that differentiated the true prophet from the false prophet was that the false prophet always gave the interpretation that the people wanted to hear. The true prophet gave the true interpretation, even if that interpretation was bad news. Joseph told the baker that in three days, Pharaoh would lift the baker's head off his body and hang him on a tree. Good news for the cupbearer; bad news for the baker.

On the third day, which was Pharaoh's birthday, he made a feast for all his servants and lifted up the head of the chief cupbearer and the head of the chief baker among his servants. He restored the chief cupbearer to his position, and he placed the cup in Pharaoh's hand. But he hanged the chief baker, as Joseph had interpreted to them. Yet the chief cupbearer did not remember Joseph, but forgot him. (vv. 20–23)

The cupbearer was elated by his good fortune. He was restored by Pharaoh, just as Joseph had predicted. When he was once again in a position of power, one in which he had the ear of Pharaoh, however, he forgot Joseph. How could he have forgotten? Perhaps he meant to tell Pharaoh about Joseph, but the time was never right. Days passed into weeks, and weeks passed into months. Life in the prison was forgotten, and Joseph was forgotten with it.

# 8

# The Timing
# of God's Providence

One of the most difficult things in life is to have hope taken away. Joseph had asked the chief cupbearer to remember him when the cupbearer was restored to his position in the palace. He asked the cupbearer to tell Pharaoh that he was innocent. Yet when the cupbearer was restored to the right hand of Pharaoh, he forgot Joseph, and so Joseph continued to languish in the dungeon.

Consider for a moment what that must have been like. It had been many years since Joseph had been sold by his brothers, and God still had not rescued him. In fact, his plight had gone from bad to worse. Now, for the first time, there seemed to be a glimmer of hope. He had someone to plead his case with Pharaoh.

Yet more time had passed, and Joseph didn't hear a word from Pharaoh's court. He'd now spent many years in exile, away from his family and everything that was precious to him. Still, Scripture tells us that God "was with Joseph" (Gen. 39:21). It was surely difficult to see that from Joseph's vantage point. As we look at the life of Joseph, however, we see beautiful, poignant insights into the providence of God and how He moves mysteriously to bring about His redemption in ways that we would never anticipate—and often in ways that include irony.

> After two whole years, Pharaoh dreamed that he was standing by the Nile. (Gen. 41:1)

A strand of irony runs through Joseph's life. At the beginning of the Joseph narrative, a dream results in his being taken to Egypt, where he eventually lands in jail. The next dreams are those of the cupbearer and the baker. After interpreting the cupbearer's dream, Joseph thought he would be released from prison, but the cupbearer forgot him. Now Pharaoh himself has a dream.

> And behold, there came up out of the Nile seven cows, attractive and plump, and they fed in the reed grass. And behold, seven other cows, ugly and thin, came up out of the Nile after them, and stood by the other cows on the bank of the Nile. And the ugly, thin cows ate up the seven attractive, plump cows. And Pharaoh awoke. And he fell asleep and dreamed a second time. And behold, seven ears of grain, plump and good, were growing on one stalk. And behold, after them sprouted seven ears, thin and blighted by the east wind. And the thin ears swallowed up the seven plump, full ears. And Pharaoh awoke, and behold, it was a dream. (vv. 2–7)

There are a couple of things to note about these dreams. First, the two dreams seem to have no relationship to each other on the surface. One is about cows and the other about stalks of wheat. Second, there is a commonality: there are fat cows and skinny cows, plump wheat and dried wheat. Both dreams involve a contrast in which something appears that seems good and something appears that seems bad. Both dreams have this negative and frightening image. It would not be immediately clear to any magician what the specific significance of these dreams was—only that the dreams had good news and bad news somehow mixed together.

The fact that there were two dreams is significant because we remember that in Scripture, repetition brings emphasis. Not only that, but truth is to be confirmed by two witnesses. So Pharaoh had repetition in his dream, and he had the confirmation that it was a troubling message by virtue of the dual witness to it. As a result, he was troubled.

> So in the morning his spirit was troubled, and he sent and called for all the magicians of Egypt and all its wise men. Pharaoh told them his dreams, but there was none who could interpret them to Pharaoh. (v. 8)

Pharaoh's reaction the next morning is exactly the same as the reaction of the cupbearer and the baker. He was terrified by the dreams, and he called for all his magicians and interpreters. None of them could interpret the dreams. But Pharaoh did have a man in his court who had once heard this message raised in the form of a question: "Do not interpretations belong to God?" (40:8). The cupbearer whose tongue had been silent for two years, who had failed to do what he said he would do when he promised to tell Pharaoh about Joseph's plight, suddenly remembered Joseph.

> Then the chief cupbearer said to Pharaoh, "I remember my offenses today. When Pharaoh was angry with his servants and put me and the chief baker in custody in the house of the captain of the guard, we dreamed on the same night, he and I, each having a dream with its own interpretation. A young Hebrew was there with us, a servant of the captain of the guard. When we told him, he interpreted our dreams to us, giving an interpretation to each man according to his dream. And as he

interpreted to us, so it came about. I was restored to my office, and the baker was hanged." (Gen. 41:9–13)

This man had forgotten Joseph, or perhaps he was afraid to mention Joseph to Pharaoh, lest in doing so he end up in Pharaoh's disfavor again. The perfect opportunity then arose for him to keep his promise. Now he was at no risk to tell Pharaoh about Joseph. In fact, he could be a hero to Pharaoh because Pharaoh was beside himself. He was distressed by these dreams, and none of his court magicians could help him. So the cupbearer stepped up and said: "Pharaoh, I think I can help you. There's a fellow in the prison who has the gift of interpreting dreams." He finally remembered Joseph.

# 9

# From Prison to Prominence

After years of trial and tribulation, Joseph was to be vindicated. The story continues in Genesis 41:

Then Pharaoh sent and called Joseph, and they quickly brought him out of the pit. And when he had shaved himself and changed his clothes, he came in before Pharaoh. And Pharaoh said to Joseph, "I have had a dream, and there is no one who can interpret it. I have heard it said of you that when you hear a dream you can interpret it."

Joseph answered Pharaoh, "It is not in me; God will give Pharaoh a favorable answer." (vv. 14–16)

The detail is added that Joseph was given a new set of clothes, because the clothes that he wore in prison were not fitting to appear before Pharaoh. Additionally, it was the custom for Egyptian men during this period of history to be clean-shaven.

Upon meeting Pharaoh, the first thing that Joseph did was to express profound humility. Pharaoh, the king of Egypt, was talking to Joseph. Joseph had just been taken out of jail. He was in exile; he was nothing in this land. Yet Pharaoh was at his wits' end; he was asking Joseph to help him.

Joseph said that he didn't have the innate ability to interpret Pharaoh's dreams. Only God could interpret the dreams. Joseph bore witness to Pharaoh of the character of his God. At the same time, he told Pharaoh that he would give him the answer. God would interpret this dream to give Pharaoh peace.

Pharaoh then recounted his dreams of the cows and the grain to Joseph. And Joseph responded by saying, "The dreams of Pharaoh are one" (v. 25). This fact had obviously been missed by Pharaoh's magicians and wise men. It wasn't two dreams; it was one dream. It was the same message given in two different forms. Joseph recognized God's handiwork of confirming the truth by repetition, and he noted a unified message in both dreams. Joseph told Pharaoh:

> "God has revealed to Pharaoh what he is about to do. The seven good cows are seven years, and the seven good ears are seven years; the dreams are one. The seven lean and ugly cows that came up after them are seven years, and the seven empty ears blighted by the east wind are also seven years of famine. It is as I told Pharaoh; God has shown to Pharaoh what he is about to do. There will come seven years of great plenty throughout all the land of Egypt, but after them there will arise seven years of famine, and all the plenty will be forgotten in the land of Egypt. The famine will consume the land, and the plenty will be unknown in the land by reason of the famine that will follow, for it will

be very severe. And the doubling of Pharaoh's dream means that the thing is fixed by God, and God will shortly bring it about." (vv. 25–32)

Joseph interpreted the dream. The cows and the wheat picture what would unfold in the nation of Egypt—seven years of plenty followed by seven years of great distress and famine. Famine can do terrible things to a nation. In those days, there were no relief agencies from wealthy nations to transport goods and food to countries in distress. When a famine came to that agricultural society, not for one year but seven years, it would be worse than the bubonic plague. Life itself would be threatened in the land. Joseph continued:

"Now therefore let Pharaoh select a discerning and wise man, and set him over the land of Egypt. Let Pharaoh proceed to appoint overseers over the land and take one-fifth of the produce of the land of Egypt during the seven plentiful years. And let them gather all the food of these good years that are coming and store up grain under the authority of Pharaoh for food in the cities, and let them keep it. That food shall be a reserve for the land against the seven years of famine that are to occur in the land of Egypt, so that the land may not perish through the famine." (vv. 33–36)

Joseph gave the word of God to the strongest politician on earth and told him that now was the time to introduce emergency measures. He told Pharaoh that in each of the seven years of plenty, a special tax should be imposed. This was no ordinary tax, but a crisis tax of 20 percent. Twenty percent of everything grown in the first seven years was to be set aside in store cities as a reserve so that Egypt could meet the crisis of the famine when it came.

He also counseled Pharaoh to appoint an able administrator to oversee the process. We shouldn't assume that Joseph was subtly suggesting himself. This was not a time for political machinations or chicanery. Joseph had the well-being of the people in view.

The ruler is responsible to be a steward, to look after the well-being of his people in part by making provisions for the future. That does not happen by spending more than you make. Every government on earth today could learn something from this text. We are a world of wasteful consumers who exploit the goods and resources of the land and don't preserve things for the future. Our silos are empty as we spend and spend. The more we tax, the more we spend.

The rationing program that Joseph advocated is similar to what occurred during World War II. There was a national emergency, and people saved lard, silk, paper, and other supplies so that there could be a future for the nation. The people understood that sacrifice was needed for survival because we were engaged in an existential conflict. Those kinds of severe situations call for sacrifices to be made in order to protect the future of the land and the people. This was no different from what God was calling Pharaoh to do. And Scripture tells us that

> this proposal pleased Pharaoh and all his servants. And Pharaoh said to his servants, "Can we find a man like this, in whom is the Spirit of God?" Then

Pharaoh said to Joseph, "Since God has shown you all this, there is none so discerning and wise as you are. You shall be over my house, and all my people shall order themselves as you command. Only as regards the throne will I be greater than you." And Pharaoh said to Joseph, "See, I have set you over all the land of Egypt." (vv. 37–41)

When God vindicated His servant, He did it far above and beyond anything that Joseph could have asked or thought. That is God. That is the promise that's made again and again in the New Testament: if we are willing to endure suffering and humiliation for a season, God has promised a future for His people beyond what the eye has seen, the ear has heard, or the heart has imagined (see 1 Cor. 2:9). We can't imagine the wondrous things that God has in store for His people who trust Him in times of languishing in prison.

God's sovereign providence displays irony again here. Joseph originally got into trouble because as a boy, he told his brothers his dream that one day he would be exalted over them. He got into trouble with his parents when he said that a time was coming when he would be exalted over them. That was only one family, however. Now, Pharaoh was putting Joseph over everyone in the kingdom except Pharaoh himself.

> Then Pharaoh took his signet ring from his hand and put it on Joseph's hand, and clothed him in garments of fine linen and put a gold chain about his neck. And he made him ride in his second chariot. And they called out before him, "Bow the knee!" Thus he set him over all the land of Egypt. (Gen. 41:42–43)

All these symbols of power were transferred to Joseph. It's not that Pharaoh instructed a craftsman to make a ring just like his so that Joseph could have one too. No, Pharaoh took off his own signet ring—the sign of his unique royal authority—and put it on Joseph's hand. He gave him garments of fine linen, the garments of royalty in Egypt. The royal garments were white in Egypt rather than the purple in some of the other ancient kingdoms—fine white linen. And Joseph received his own private chariot. In the royal procession, Pharaoh drove in the first chariot, and the second chariot was occupied by Joseph, who was second-in-command in the whole nation.

This all may seem extreme and extravagant, and we might think that Pharaoh was acting a bit impetuously. We must realize, however, that Joseph had just saved the kingdom. Pharaoh would have been king over nothing in fourteen years without Joseph. He would have been unprepared for the devastating famine that would have destroyed his land. Not only that, but he would still be trying to figure out the meaning of the mysterious dreams he'd had.

Obviously, Pharaoh was initially inclined to think that Joseph might possess an extraordinary degree of wisdom, making him useful in the position of power and authority that would be needed to save the nation. But he was also getting more information about Joseph and learning that Joseph's track record was one of unparalleled excellence in administration. He had found his man.

It's also important to understand that Joseph was not only made the head of peacetime operations in the land; he was also in charge of war. He was the chief executive officer for domestic concerns, but he was also the commander in chief of the armies of Egypt. All that responsibility was given to a slave taken from a dungeon. That's God. That's what God does when He raises up whom He will and brings the mighty down from their thrones. That's the power we see displayed in the life of Joseph.

# 10

# Feast and Famine

After interpreting Pharaoh's dream and proposing a plan to sustain the nation, Joseph was elevated to second-in-command in Egypt. We read in Genesis 41:

> And Pharaoh called Joseph's name Zaphenath-paneah. And he gave him in marriage Asenath, the daughter of Potiphera priest of On. So Joseph went out over the land of Egypt. (v. 45)

The meaning of the Egyptian name given to Joseph is unclear, but most commentators understand it to mean "God speaks and He lives." If this is the true meaning, the name would be a powerful acknowledgment by Pharaoh that Joseph's ability to interpret dreams came from God—and an acknowledgment of Joseph's God.

Then we read that Pharaoh gave Asenath to Joseph in marriage, and her name means "belonging to the goddess Neith." Some have suggested that perhaps this is an overt sin in Joseph's life, since he took for his wife a woman named after a pagan Egyptian goddess. Further, they say that Joseph was violating God's laws of marriage by entering into a union with a woman who was not, presumably, a believer in the Hebrew faith.

In the Old Testament, however, this kind of thing happened regularly. The patriarchs, on various occasions, took wives from other nations, but these women became faithful in their service to Yahweh. We may assume that the woman whom Joseph married came under his tutelage and became a true daughter of Yahweh.

She is also called "the daughter of Potiphera," or Potiphar. That raises some interesting speculation, since the only other time we see this name in the Genesis narrative is with respect to the captain of the guard whose wife leveled the false accusation against Joseph that resulted in his being thrown into prison. There's no reason to assume, however, that the Potiphar mentioned in this text is the same Potiphar who had bought Joseph and put him over his house. Just as in our day, people in the ancient world often had the same name, and this particular Potiphar is identified as a priest rather than as the captain of Pharaoh's guard.

According to verse 46, Joseph was thirty years old when he stood before Pharaoh, king of Egypt. This means that thirteen years had passed since Joseph was sold into slavery by his brothers. It took a long time for the invisible hand of providence to rescue Joseph from the ordeals that he suffered. John Knox, the great Scottish Reformer, spent more than a year as a galley slave before he was freed and rose to the position of leader of the Reformation in Scotland. Yet Knox's time of incarceration isn't worthy to be compared with the sufferings endured by Joseph. Joseph wasn't in prison for all thirteen of those years, but he had been in exile, either as a slave or imprisoned.

Joseph went out from the presence of Pharaoh
and went through all the land of Egypt. During
the seven plentiful years the earth produced abun-
dantly, and he gathered up all the food of these
seven years, which occurred in the land of Egypt,
and put the food in the cities. He put in every city
the food from the fields around it. And Joseph
stored up grain in great abundance, like the sand
of the sea, until he ceased to measure it, for it could
not be measured. (vv. 46–49)

Here we see the fulfillment of Pharaoh's dream in
the seven years of bountiful harvest. During that seven-
year period, Joseph established store cities and built up
enormous reserve supplies of grain to guard against the
impending famine.

Before the year of famine came, two sons were
born to Joseph. Asenath, the daughter of Potiphera
priest of On, bore them to him. Joseph called the
name of the firstborn Manasseh. "For," he said,
"God has made me forget all my hardship and all

my father's house." The name of the second he called Ephraim, "For God has made me fruitful in the land of my affliction." (vv. 50–52)

Critics of Joseph have raised serious concerns about this episode of the naming of his two sons. Before addressing this, let's remember that these two sons became extremely prominent in biblical history. Joseph's father, Jacob, had twelve sons, and from those twelve sons descended the twelve tribes of Israel. When God numbered the people and divided the land after the exodus, He apportioned territories according to the tribes to which the people belonged. Yet there was no tribe of Joseph. Rather, Joseph's portion was divided between his two sons, Manasseh and Ephraim.

Those tribes became two of the most important tribes in the subsequent history of Israel. With respect to their names, we are told that Joseph called his first-born Manasseh, which means "making forgetful." Joseph explained this name by saying, "God has made me forget all my hardship and all my father's house" (v. 51). Is Joseph saying that because of this great boon that he received from Pharaoh—his new life and exaltation to a position of authority—he could forget his former troubles, his family, his father's house, and his heritage?

The worst-case analysis would be that Joseph had abandoned his faith in the promises that he had received from God as a boy. That would be an extremely jarring surprise in light of everything we've learned so far about Joseph's character. Certainly the rest of the narrative belies that conclusion. Likely, Joseph was simply saying that he could now forget that he was cut off altogether from his family because God had given him a family of his own. He now had a son. God had given him a new family.

This doesn't mean that he was repudiating his old family, but his family before this time was the only family he had. That was troublesome to him because during his years of suffering, he had no family present. Now he did. He had a wife, he had a son, and he was going to have another son, as the text indicates. He named his second son Ephraim, meaning "fruitfulness," and said, "For God has made me fruitful in the land of my affliction" (v. 52).

That statement summarizes the story of Joseph's life, and it highlights the significance of his story for us because it is a history of affliction upon affliction that ends in divine reward and divine grace. God allowed Joseph to bear fruit amid his seemingly barren life experience. Out of that affliction came great fruitfulness. In a sense, the highest way that Joseph could show his gratitude to God for vindicating him and giving him sweet fruit out of what had been nothing but a bitter providence is seen in the name of his second son.

> The seven years of plenty that occurred in the land of Egypt came to an end, and the seven years of famine began to come, as Joseph had said. There was famine in all lands, but in all the land of Egypt there was bread. When all the land of Egypt was famished, the people cried to Pharaoh for bread. Pharaoh said to all the Egyptians, "Go to Joseph. What he says to you, do."
>
> So when the famine had spread over all the land, Joseph opened all the storehouses and sold to the Egyptians, for the famine was severe in the land of Egypt. Moreover, all the earth came to Egypt to Joseph to buy grain, because the famine was severe over all the earth. (vv. 53–57)

When Joseph stored up the grain, he did so without measure. When the famine came—as severe as it was—not only was there enough grain to feed the people of Egypt during those seven years, but people from other countries came to buy whatever they could from the Egyptians. That detail sets the stage for why Joseph's brothers would migrate south, coming down to Egypt to buy some food. It had become known throughout the world that one nation had been able to survive the famine—Egypt.

When this seven-year famine began, the people of other nations obviously didn't know that the famine would last that long, so they did not take the elaborate measures that Egypt did to store up reserves. If we reason that there was a modicum of judicial responsibility in other lands, however, we can't assume that those lands completely consumed all the resources they had received over the seven years of plenty. The people in these other nations wouldn't suddenly have been starving in the first six months of the famine. They would have had a certain amount of reserve, though not as much as the Egyptians had.

Therefore, we can't assume that on the first day of the second set of seven years, Joseph opened all the storehouses and started distributing the grain. He had to manage the stores in such a way that the resources would be distributed over a seven-year period. We must keep in mind that the famine increased in severity over time. One year of famine is one problem, but it compounds when the year after a year of famine is another year of famine—and then the third year, the fourth year, the fifth year, and so on.

As time passed, the problem of hunger around the world became intense and severe. After a period of time, people came from other nations, seeking relief from the Egyptians. "Moreover, all the earth came to Egypt to Joseph to buy grain, because the famine was severe over all the earth" (v. 57).

Chapter 42 begins:

When Jacob learned that there was grain for sale in Egypt, he said to his sons, "Why do you look at one another?" And he said, "Behold, I have heard that there is grain for sale in Egypt. Go down and buy grain for us there, that we may live and not die." (vv. 1–2)

These are rather harsh words from Jacob. His sons worked the family homestead. They had been taking care of the flocks when Joseph was sent out to check on them earlier in the narrative. What happened to the flocks?

It wasn't just people who suffered from the loss of grain. The livestock became the first casualties in the severe famine and drought. We see this even today. When droughts occur, there are terrible problems with the loss of livestock. The first ones to go are the animals.

Jacob was advanced in years. His sons were responsible for providing the household with food, and they were doing nothing. Jacob took charge of the situation and told them to go down to Egypt and buy grain so that they wouldn't die of starvation. Jacob still had money; what he didn't have was food. You can't eat money.

Jacob and his family were in a dire situation, and the famine set the stage for the dramatic encounter that would come to pass between Joseph and his long-lost brothers.

# 11

# The Meeting

We come now to the dramatic moment in the narrative of Joseph's life when he meets his brothers again. Joseph was seventeen when they betrayed him, and he became prime minister of Egypt at the age of thirty. Thirteen years had passed between his being sold into slavery and his becoming prime minister, and to that we must add the seven years of plenty. Joseph's brothers didn't come immediately at the beginning of the seven years of famine, so more than twenty years had elapsed since these men had seen each other.

# JOSEPH

We read in Genesis 42:

> So ten of Joseph's brothers went down to buy
> grain in Egypt. But Jacob did not send Benjamin,
> Joseph's brother, with his brothers, for he feared
> that harm might happen to him. (vv. 3–4)

Jacob had wanted to marry Rachel, but her father,
Laban, insisted that Jacob serve him for seven years
before giving Rachel to Jacob in marriage. Jacob did
so, and at the end of that time, Laban deceitfully gave
Rachel's older sister, Leah, to Jacob in marriage. It was
shameful in that culture for the younger daughter to be
married ahead of the older daughter, so Laban tricked
Jacob. Laban then insisted that Jacob work another
seven years for Rachel. In all, Jacob worked for his
father-in-law for fourteen years to get Rachel.

Though Jacob had children through Leah and
through his concubines Bilhah and Zilpah, Rachel was
the real love of his life. He longed to have offspring
from her, but initially she was barren. When her womb
was finally opened, she brought forth a son. Her first

son was Joseph, and her second son was Benjamin. Benjamin was the youngest of the sons of Jacob, and Jacob doted on Benjamin even more than he had on Joseph. Not only that, but great pain came to the household of Jacob with the birth of Benjamin—due to complications from that birth, Rachel died.

Jacob was willing to risk his other ten sons, but he wasn't willing to risk Benjamin. He sent the ten on this rugged journey to Egypt, but he wouldn't let Benjamin leave home. He wanted to protect him. Some interpreters have said that this indicates a lack of faith on Jacob's part—that Jacob was not like Abraham, the father of the faithful, who went wherever God told him to go and trusted in His promises. By contrast, Jacob, who had the promises of God for his sons, waffled in his faith.

The biblical patriarchs were men of flesh and blood, and a mixture of fear and doubt always diluted the purity of their confidence in the promises of God. We may have expected Jacob to say, "I'll risk all my boys, because after all, I'm entrusting them to the providence of God," but he was not prepared to do that.

But Jacob did not send Benjamin, Joseph's brother, with his brothers, for he feared that harm might happen to him. Thus the sons of Israel came to buy among the others who came, for the famine was in the land of Canaan. Now Joseph was governor over the land. He was the one who sold to all the people of the land. And Joseph's brothers came and bowed themselves before him with their faces to the ground. (vv. 4–6)

Already we see the beginning of the fulfillment of the dream that had gotten Joseph into so much trouble with his brothers in the first place. More than twenty years later, that dream was being fulfilled as they came and prostrated themselves before him. They didn't know that they were bowing down before their brother Joseph. All they knew was that they were in the presence of the prime minister of Egypt, and they certainly didn't expect that the prime minister was Joseph. They assumed that Joseph was dead.

We may wonder why the brothers didn't recognize him. First, many years had passed. A lot of changes had taken place in Joseph, who was now in his thirties or forties. Not only that, but he was attired in the garb of the Egyptians. He was clean-shaven. He was wearing the opulent trappings of the palace. These factors would work to conceal his identity from his brothers. In this encounter, Joseph was careful not to speak to them in his own language but communicated to them through an interpreter. This was another way to conceal his identity from them.

We read in verse 8, "Joseph recognized his brothers, but they did not recognize him." What a moment that must have been. Joseph was busy administering the reserve grain program for his people when his brothers appeared. He recognized them instantly. Can you imagine the jolt to his soul that this episode produced? Yet he retained his composure and initiated a program of playacting that involved shrewd deception.

This has provoked some to criticize Joseph and call him a liar. Yet Martin Luther had an interesting insight into this episode. He did not see in Joseph's elaborately conceived plan a game of sinfulness or even a game of vengeance. Instead, he likened it to what God often does with us. It's similar to what parents do when they discipline their children. Every parent knows what it means to feign greater anger with their children than they possess for the purpose of disciplining them. We do this to awaken them to the seriousness of the matter.

Even as God chastens those whom He loves and shows us the divine frown, Luther calls this a sweet and heavenly game. Not a game in the frivolous sense, but a game in the sense that God is pretending to be more distressed with us than He actually is. It is for a redemptive purpose, to bring us to repentance, just as the parent scolds the child to bring that child to an awakening and to an awareness of what is right and wrong. This is how Luther describes the game that Joseph was playing.

Joseph was concerned about several things here. First, he wanted to find out the status of his father. Second, he wanted to find out the status of his brother Benjamin. Third, he wanted his brothers to come to a knowledge of truth and godliness. So exercising his authority as the prime minister, he did not immediately reveal himself to his brothers but instead engaged in a calculated deception.

Notice what happened here initially. We are told that "Joseph saw his brothers and recognized them, but he treated them like strangers and spoke roughly to them" (v. 7). We know that he still loved them, for we see in subsequent passages that his heart melts, he goes into another room, and he weeps over his brothers. Yet here, he deliberately spoke harshly to them, acting like a stranger.

"'Where do you come from?' he said" (v. 7). He knew where they came from. Didn't God Himself say to Adam, "Where are you?" (3:9). God knew where Adam was, but He acted as though He didn't know for His own divine purposes of reproof and sanctification in Adam's and Eve's lives. Joseph acted in a similar manner. The brothers replied, "From the land of Canaan, to buy food" (42:7). This was the first truthful thing they had said to Joseph in a long time. So far, they were speaking the truth.

"And Joseph recognized his brothers, but they did not recognize him. And Joseph remembered the dreams that he had dreamed of them" (vv. 8–9). How did Joseph reply to his brothers? Did he say: "You are my long-lost brothers, and you just bowed down before me, fulfilling that dream I told you about so long ago. Now let's all be friends"? No, that's not what he said. Instead, "he said to them, 'You are spies; you have come to see the nakedness of the land'" (v. 9).

In other words, Joseph was saying, "You've come from some enemy nation to spy out Egypt to see how weakened we are by the ravages of this famine." That's a reasonable element of this deception. The brothers would have understood why the prime minister may have been suspicious of them. Rather than a single representative's coming to make the request, ten Hebrews had come to the court of Egypt, saying that they wanted to purchase food.

> They said to him, "No, my lord, your servants have come to buy food. We are all sons of one man. We are honest men. Your servants have never been spies."
>
> He said to them, "No, it is the nakedness of the land that you have come to see." And they said, "We, your servants, are twelve brothers, the sons of one

man in the land of Canaan, and behold, the youngest is this day with our father, and one is no more."
(vv. 10–13)

Here we have truth mixed with lies. "We are all sons
of one man"—that's true. "We are honest men"—that's
not true. "Your servants have never been spies"—that
is true. Yet they inadvertently revealed information to
Joseph that he desperately wanted to hear. Now he knew
that his brother Benjamin was still alive. He also realized
that they were assuming that he, Joseph, was dead.

But Joseph said to them, "It is as I said to you. You
are spies. By this you shall be tested: by the life of
Pharaoh, you shall not go from this place unless
your youngest brother comes here. Send one of you,
and let him bring your brother, while you remain
confined, that your words may be tested, whether
there is truth in you. Or else, by the life of Pharaoh,
surely you are spies." And he put them all together
in custody for three days. (vv. 14–17)

It would have been perfectly legitimate for Joseph to simply put them all in jail and let them rot for the same amount of time that he had been in jail because of their actions. Instead, he put them in prison for three days.

> On the third day Joseph said to them, "Do this and you will live, for I fear God: if you are honest men, let one of your brothers remain confined where you are in custody, and let the rest go and carry grain for the famine of your households, and bring your youngest brother to me. So your words will be verified, and you shall not die." (vv. 18–20)

Joseph changed the terms of the test. He had previously said that only one of them could go home while the rest stayed in prison. Then he said that only one of them needed to stay and the rest could go home.

Joseph feigned anger and distrust toward his brothers as potential spies even though he knew who they were and was not truly angry with them. In so doing, in one sense, he mirrored the way that God sometimes manifests Himself to us. Have you ever assumed that God was so angry with you that there was nothing you could possibly do to assuage His wrath and restore a right relationship with Him? It's important for us as Christians to understand the chastening of God.

Even when we come under God's discipline and He appears to have a frown on His face, we must understand that even His discipline is a manifestation of His care for us as His children. We know that from the Word of God. So we ought never to despair, even when we fall into sin and approach God with repentant hearts. This is what His chastening is designed to make us do. We ought not to be afraid of the permanent anger of God; rather, we should be confident in the knowledge that He loves us.

# 12

# The Test

After many years of separation, Joseph's brothers appeared before him, seeking grain from Egypt. They did not recognize him, so Joseph concealed his true identity from them. Not only that, but he accused them of being spies who had come to assess the weakness of Egypt. He first said that he would keep nine of them in prison while one went back home to retrieve Benjamin and to prove that they were not spies. But after three days, he showed grace toward them by saying that he would keep only one in Egypt and that the rest could journey home and bring Benjamin to Egypt.

We pick up the story in Genesis 42:

> Then they said to one another, "In truth we are guilty
> concerning our brother, in that we saw the distress of
> his soul, when he begged us and we did not listen.
> That is why this distress has come upon us." (v. 21)

Suddenly, the brothers were made freshly aware of their abiding guilt—the blood that was on their hands from betraying Joseph so many years earlier. They weren't saying this directly to Joseph. Rather, they were talking among themselves in his presence, assuming that since he was speaking to them through a translator, he didn't understand what they were saying.

Notice that the guilt and the stricken consciences of these men had not been relieved for more than twenty years. They were still haunted by the blood of their brother on their hands—and not only the betrayal of Joseph but the dreadful betrayal of their father, to whom they had lied about this incident.

They had watched Jacob's grief and anguish when they reported to him that Joseph had been slain by a wild animal. They had kept this deception from Jacob all these years, but it was still bothering them. Like the pagan who trembles at the rustling of a leaf when meeting his first adversity, they were afraid that they were reaping their just rewards. They feared that they were experiencing the vengeance of God for their sin through what was happening with this powerful ruler of Egypt.

Sin is a burden to carry. Joseph's brothers were bearing a burden of guilt that had not been forgiven or redeemed, and it was haunting them. We must not assume that unbelieving, impenitent sinners, even though they may acquire a hardness of heart or stiffness of neck, are left without any conscience. The conscience is still God's inner voice by which even unbelievers are accused of their sin. It does not bring them to true repentance, but it does bring them to fear—to being frightened of the judgment of God. In the perilous situation before the stern prime minister of Egypt, who was accusing them of being spies and threatening to keep one of them in prison, Joseph's brothers began to talk among themselves honestly.

They were not trying to conceal from one another their treachery from years ago. They all knew that they had engaged in this conspiracy against Joseph. They were admitting their guilt, which is one of the hardest things for a human being to do. As fallen people, even when we are clear in our own minds about our guilt, we try, like Lady Macbeth, to wash that stain from our hands, to remove the spot and blemish from our souls—but we can't do it.

So we lie to ourselves and conceal from ourselves and from everyone else what we really are, because "the heart is deceitful above all things, and desperately sick" (Jer. 17:9). The heart is deceitfully wicked to such a degree that we deceive even ourselves. We don't want to face up to the reality of our sin. That reluctance to face the stark nakedness of our actual guilt is not suddenly erased from our souls with our conversion. Even King David, a godly man, had to be directly charged by the prophet Nathan to face up to his crime. Even as believers, we find it difficult to admit our sins.

Joseph's older brothers were acknowledging their guilt, but they were not acknowledging it openly. They were acknowledging it only among themselves because they were co-conspirators in the crime. They were terrified. They likely sensed the judgment of God on their heads.

> And Reuben answered them, "Did I not tell you not to sin against the boy? But you did not listen. So now there comes a reckoning for his blood." (Gen. 42:22)

Don't think too highly of Reuben for this. He was covering his own tracks. He said, "I told you not to do that," but he had been a co-conspirator for more than two decades. He had withheld the truth from his father. He was as guilty as the rest of them in this crime, but now he tried to save his own skin. He was trying to sound self-righteous before his brothers.

> They did not know that Joseph understood them, for there was an interpreter between them. Then he turned away from them and wept. (vv. 23–24)

Just imagine the pain that Joseph experienced in hearing his brothers acknowledge what they had done to him. Joseph began to weep uncontrollably and had to leave their presence so that he could pour out his grief. If Joseph had burst into tears in front of his brothers, that would have been the end of his cleverly designed game plan. So he left.

> And he returned to them and spoke to them. And he took Simeon from them and bound him before their eyes. And Joseph gave orders to fill their bags with grain, and to replace every man's money in his sack, and to give them provisions for the journey. This was done for them. Then they loaded their donkeys with their grain and departed. (vv. 24–26)

Of course, they didn't know that Joseph had commanded that the money they used to pay for the grain be returned to their sacks. This was all part of Joseph's carefully crafted scheme to trap his brothers and to lead them into a full acknowledgment of their sin.

> And as one of them opened his sack to give his donkey fodder at the lodging place, he saw his money in the mouth of his sack. He said to his brothers, "My

money has been put back; here it is in the mouth of my sack!" At this their hearts failed them, and they turned trembling to one another, saying, "What is this that God has done to us?" (vv. 27–28)

They were journeying home. When they stopped for the night and took off the packs from the backs of the beasts, one of the brothers checked his bag and found his money in it. Notice that the brothers did not say, "What is this that the prime minister has done to us?" Rather, they said, "What is this that God has done to us?" They saw the significance.

Consequently, Scripture says, "Their hearts failed them" (v. 28). These men had been pretty bold even in their sin, but now their boldness vanished and their hearts failed in their terror about the repercussions of this incident.

When they came to Jacob their father in the land of Canaan, they told him all that had happened to them, saying, "The man, the lord of the land, spoke roughly to us and took us to be spies of the land. But we said to him, 'We are honest men; we have never been spies. We are twelve brothers, sons of our father. One is no more, and the youngest is this day with our father in the land of Canaan.' Then the man, the lord of the land, said to us, 'By this I shall know that you are honest men: leave one of your brothers with me, and take grain for the famine of your households, and go your way. Bring your youngest brother to me. Then I shall know that you are not spies but honest men, and I will deliver your brother to you, and you shall trade in the land.'" (vv. 29–34)

The brothers tried to calm Jacob down by putting the whole incident in the best possible light. They didn't talk about finding the money in their sacks. They just said that the prime minister had spoken some rough words to them and thought they were spies, but they could get the grain if they just met the terms of his requirements. They weren't being fully open with Jacob about how terrified they were to go back. They were afraid of what would happen to them when the prime minister of Egypt discovered that one of them still had the money for the grain.

# 13

# It's Not
# as It Seems

Terror entered the hearts of Joseph's brothers when they found money in one of their sacks of grain. Now the Egyptian prime minister would accuse them not only of being spies but also of being thieves. As a result, when they told their story to Jacob, they left out that detail.

The story continues in Genesis 42:35–36:

As they emptied their sacks, behold, every man's bundle of money was in his sack. And when they and their father saw their bundles of money, they were afraid. And Jacob their father said to them, "You have bereaved me of my children: Joseph is no more, and Simeon is no more, and now you would take Benjamin. All this has come against me."

Jacob expressed his profound grief. This patriarch who had received the promises of God and the patriarchal blessing was now driven to despair.

The hand of providence is invisible. We don't know what God is doing below the surface of the things that we can perceive with our eyes. Hidden beneath the visible lies the invisible rule of God.

It's hard for us as Christians to trust our lives and our futures to an invisible reign, because things are not always as they appear to be. That's what it means to "walk by faith, not by sight" (2 Cor. 5:7), because sometimes our sight gives us no hope whatsoever for the future. At this point, Jacob was walking by sight. He was human, and he was responding in the flesh. He was responding to what he knew. He was responding to the facts as he had perceived them.

Yet Jacob was not making a hasty assumption. Why

would he not reasonably assume that Joseph was no more? He hadn't been an eyewitness to Joseph's death, but his sons had come back and testified as a group that they were eyewitnesses. Not only that, but they had given forensic evidence by presenting the mutilated coat that was covered with blood.

Why did Jacob assume that Simeon was also no more? Just as the brothers had returned years ago without Joseph, they had now come back from Egypt with the story of this harsh ruler who had thrown Jacob's son Simeon into prison. Once they found the money in the bags, Jacob likely had little hope of ever seeing Simeon again. If Simeon was being held as a test to see whether the brothers were honorable men, coming home with all the money in their bags would show that they were dishonorable and untrustworthy. As a result, Jacob reasoned that Simeon, like Joseph, was no more. He said, "All this has come against me." What had happened to his faith in the promises of God? At this moment, his faith was at a low ebb, and he was walking by sight and not by faith.

Never in Jacob's life had the providence of God been more singularly focused on his immediate welfare than at the very moment when he said, "Everything is against me." Because at that moment, he was actually on the threshold of finding his son who he thought was dead, of being reunited with the son he loved so much, and of having his family redeemed from the ravages of the famine. All that was about to happen in a very short time because God had so ordered the affairs of history to bring everything together for Jacob and his family. Yet from his vantage point, all that Jacob could see was that everything was against him.

> Then Reuben said to his father, "Kill my two sons if I do not bring [Benjamin] back to you. Put him in my hands, and I will bring him back to you." But he said, "My son shall not go down with you, for his brother is dead, and he is the only one left. If harm should happen to him on the journey that you are to make, you would bring down my gray hairs with sorrow to Sheol." (Gen. 42:37–38)

Reuben's suggestion was inappropriate, and Jacob rejected it. He had no hope for Simeon, but he still had hope for Benjamin. At this point, the clock speeds up a bit in the narrative:

> Now the famine was severe in the land. And when they had eaten the grain that they had brought from Egypt, their father said to them, "Go again, buy us a little food." (43:1–2)

In Genesis 42, in response to Reuben's pleas, Jacob said that they were never going back to Egypt. He wasn't letting Benjamin go there. They were staying as far away from Egypt as they could. Then something happened to change his mind.

The brothers had accomplished their original mission, though not without cost. They did come back home with grain and receive at least temporary relief from the famine. When Jacob was being so obstinate about their not going down to Egypt again, perhaps he was banking that the grain would tide his family over until they were out of danger. He had to assume that the famine wouldn't last forever. The ominous statement that follows, however, is "Now the famine was severe in the land."

Instead of getting better, the famine got worse and worse, and the limited grain that they had procured on the first journey was exhausted. Jacob thus changed his mind about the brothers' returning to Egypt, but he didn't do so until the circumstances of the crisis were so intense that he really had no choice. Now the stage was set for the brothers to return to Egypt and once again come face-to-face with Joseph.

# 14

# Sitting at Joseph's Table

The more desperate the situation, the more risks we are willing to take. We see this principle on display when Jacob changed his mind about letting his sons go back to Egypt. Earlier, he had vehemently protested their suggestion of returning to Pharaoh's court to seek Simeon's release and additional grain. Jacob said no until the famine became so severe that he was left with no other option. We pick up the narrative in Genesis 43, when Jacob relented and told his sons to return to Egypt to buy them some food.

But Judah said to him, "The man solemnly warned us, saying, 'You shall not see my face unless your brother is with you.' If you will send our brother with us, we will go down and buy you food. But if you will not send him, we will not go down, for the man said to us, 'You shall not see my face, unless your brother is with you.'" (vv. 3–5)

Judah insisted that it was not good enough simply to send them back to Egypt; they had to take Benjamin along. He reminded his father of the terms established by the Egyptian prime minister—terms that they had to follow if they wanted to entertain any hope of Simeon's release. Jacob responded, "Why did you treat me so badly as to tell the man that you had another brother?" (v. 6). We can sense Jacob's anguish at the thought of risking the loss of Benjamin.

They replied, "The man questioned us carefully about ourselves and our kindred, saying, 'Is your father still alive? Do you have another brother?' What we told him was in answer to these questions.

SITTING AT JOSEPH'S TABLE

Could we in any way know that he would say, 'Bring your brother down'?" And Judah said to Israel his father, "Send the boy with me, and we will arise and go, that we may live and not die, both we and you and also our little ones. I will be a pledge of his safety. From my hand you shall require him. If I do not bring him back to you and set him before you, then let me bear the blame forever. If we had not delayed, we would now have returned twice." (vv. 7–10)

Judah essentially said: "Father, we don't have time to argue about this. If we don't go down there and take Benjamin with us, we're all going to die—not only your sons, but your grandchildren as well. So let us go; send the boy with us. I will be his surety. I will guarantee his safety with my own life."

Then their father Israel said to them, "If it must be so, then do this: take some of the choice fruits of the land in your bags, and carry a present down to the man, a little balm and a little honey, gum, myrrh, pistachio nuts, and almonds. Take double the money with you. Carry back with you the money that was returned in the mouth of your sacks. Perhaps it was an oversight. Take also your brother, and arise, go again to the man. May God Almighty grant you mercy before the man, and may he send back your other brother and Benjamin. And as for me, if I am bereaved of my children, I am bereaved." (vv. 11–14)

We have seen the patriarch Jacob's turmoil as he faced this seemingly great threat to his beloved son Benjamin. We have seen him struggling with his faith, doubting the promises that God had made so many years earlier to him, to his father, and to his grandfather. In his old age, all the promises of God now meet in this decision. Everything is at risk. This is the time for truth. Finally, we see Jacob the man of faith emerge.

This reminds me of the experience of the young men Shadrach, Meshach, and Abednego in the book of Daniel. When the king threatened to throw them into the fiery furnace, they said: "Our God whom we serve is able to deliver us from the burning fiery furnace, and he will deliver us out of your hand, O king. But if not, be it known to you, O king, that we will not serve your gods or worship the golden image that you have set up" (Dan. 3:17–18). That's faith, and that's what Jacob was saying: "I'm going to pray that God will bring a happy ending out of this, but if He doesn't, He doesn't. If I am bereaved, I am bereaved."

Many people think that the "prayer of faith" is the prayer that claims the good ending in advance and simply believes that whatever we pray for will come to pass. The true prayer of faith actually puts the request in the hands of God and trusts Him for the outcome. That's what Jacob did.

So the men took this present, and they took double the money with them, and Benjamin. They arose and went down to Egypt and stood before Joseph.

When Joseph saw Benjamin with them, he said to the steward of his house, "Bring the men into the house, and slaughter an animal and make ready, for the men are to dine with me at noon." The man did as Joseph told him and brought the men to Joseph's house. And the men were afraid because they were brought to Joseph's house, and they said, "It is because of the money, which was replaced in our sacks the first time, that we are brought in, so that he may assault us and fall upon us to make us servants and seize our donkeys." (Gen. 43:15–18)

Can you imagine the emotion that was welling up in Joseph's soul as he saw his little brother for the first time in more than twenty years? Rather than meeting with his brothers at the palace, Joseph invited them to dinner at his own house. This was the highest honor that a ruler could bestow on a guest. When the steward notified the brothers about the invitation, however, they were terrified. They wondered why he was doing this. They couldn't imagine that they were going to be honored by Joseph. The fact that this was a change from the normal place for transacting business only excited greater disquietude and apprehension in them.

So they went up to the steward of Joseph's house and spoke with him at the door of the house, and said, "Oh, my lord, we came down the first time to buy food. And when we came to the lodging place we opened our sacks, and there was each man's money in the mouth of his sack, our money in full weight. So we have brought it again with us, and we have brought other money down with us to buy food. We do not know who put our money in our sacks." (vv. 19–22)

They told the story just as Jacob had advised them to do. In effect, they said to the steward: "When we were going home last time, we were astonished to discover that the money we thought we had left behind was in our sacks. We have no idea how that happened. Here's the money, and here's a second round of the same amount. We want to make it absolutely clear to you that we have no interest in stealing anything from the Egyptians."

[The steward] replied, "Peace to you, do not be afraid. Your God and the God of your father has put treasure in your sacks for you. I received your money." (v. 23)

How often in sacred Scripture do we hear the
injunction to not be afraid coming from the lips of an
angel or from Christ Himself? Yet here it is the steward
who is the messenger of peace. The brothers must have
been beside themselves in wonder. They had been terrified since they had found that money, but here they
were being told that God had arranged for that money
to be returned to them and that they had no reason to
be afraid. Here we see that the steward, an Egyptian,
had more confidence in the providence of God than
Joseph's brothers did.

> Then he brought Simeon out to them. And when
> the man had brought the men into Joseph's house
> and given them water, and they had washed their
> feet, and when he had given their donkeys fodder,
> they prepared the present for Joseph's coming at
> noon, for they heard that they should eat bread
> there. When Joseph came home, they brought
> into the house to him the present that they had
> with them and bowed down to him to the ground.
> (vv. 23–26)

124

Here again we see the fulfillment of the dream that Joseph had as a teenager as his brothers bowed down before him.

> And he inquired about their welfare and said, "Is your father well, the old man of whom you spoke? Is he still alive?" They said, "Your servant our father is well; he is still alive." And they bowed their heads and prostrated themselves. And he lifted up his eyes and saw his brother Benjamin, his mother's son, and said, "Is this your youngest brother, of whom you spoke to me? God be gracious to you, my son!" Then Joseph hurried out, for his compassion grew warm for his brother, and he sought a place to weep. And he entered his chamber and wept there. Then he washed his face and came out. And controlling himself he said, "Serve the food." (vv. 27–31)

This is the second time that Joseph had to interrupt an interview with his brothers because he was so overcome with emotion. He had to excuse himself and go into another room to allow his tears to flow freely.

These were tears of ecstasy, tears of unbridled joy, tears of relief, to see his only full brother safe and sound and to hear that his father was not only still alive but in good health. What follows is this brief account:

> They served him by himself, and them by them-
> selves, and the Egyptians who ate with him by
> themselves, because the Egyptians could not eat
> with the Hebrews, for that is an abomination to
> the Egyptians. (v. 32)

This is a strange twist. So often in the Old Testament, it's the Jews who are prohibited from sharing table fellowship with pagans and gentiles as part of the purification rites of Judaism. In this case, in the Egyptian culture it was an abomination for the Egyptians to share this kind of fellowship with Hebrews. Remember, when Potiphar's wife brought false charges against Joseph, she said, "How could you allow this Hebrew slave to mock me in this manner?" She said this because the Hebrews were considered beneath the dignity of the Egyptians.

And they sat before him, the firstborn according
to his birthright and the youngest according to
his youth. And the men looked at one another in
amazement. Portions were taken to them from
Joseph's table, but Benjamin's portion was five
times as much as any of theirs. And they drank and
were merry with him. (vv. 33–34)

Why were the brothers amazed? Joseph had seated
his brothers in order from the firstborn to the youngest. How would the prime minister of Egypt know the
birth order of these men? They had to assume that he
possessed some magical gift or supernatural insight
that allowed him to perfectly arrange the table.

Hospitality in ancient Egypt was unlike the hospitality found in ancient Rome or in Greece. When a
king or a prince threw a feast in Rome or Greece, an
abundance of food was set before the people at the
table. Everybody gorged themselves with as much food
as they could possibly take in, and at the end, there
would always be a lot of waste. This was not the custom of the Egyptians, particularly during the famine.

Each person was given exactly the same portion, and the portion you were given was the portion you were expected to consume.

Yet when Joseph had the meal served, each person was given his allotted portion except for Benjamin, who was given a fivefold honor. Five times as much food was given to this special brother than was given to the rest. "And they drank and were merry with him" (v. 34). Now we see a new note in the atmosphere of their relationship. A note of joy is introduced. Joseph's brothers must have felt as though they were on an emotional roller coaster, but what comes next heightens the drama even more.

# 15

# The Silver Cup

As we reach this point in the narrative of Joseph's life, the plot thickens. After treating his brothers to a sumptuous feast, Joseph made provisions for their departure while he continued his work of subterfuge designed to lead them to full repentance.

> Then [Joseph] commanded the steward of his house, "Fill the men's sacks with food, as much as they can carry, and put each man's money in the mouth of his sack, and put my cup, the silver cup,

in the mouth of the sack of the youngest, with his money for the grain." And he did as Joseph told him. (Gen. 44:1–2)

This is the second time that Joseph employed a devious trick to ensnare his brothers. The first time, he returned to their sacks the money they had paid for the original grain. This time, he added a little twist. Not only did Joseph return each man's money to his sack, but he also instructed the steward to put his silver cup into Benjamin's bag. It was difficult for Jacob to allow Benjamin to go on this journey, and now the stage was set for the worst of all possible outcomes.

As soon as the morning was light, the men were sent away with their donkeys. They had gone only a short distance from the city. Now Joseph said to his steward, "Up, follow after the men, and when you overtake them, say to them, 'Why have you repaid evil for good? Is it not from this that my lord drinks, and by this that he practices divination? You have done evil in doing this.'"

When he overtook them, he spoke to them these words. They said to him, "Why does my lord speak such words as these? Far be it from your servants to do such a thing! Behold, the money that we found in the mouths of our sacks we brought back to you from the land of Canaan. How then could we steal silver or gold from your lord's house? Whichever of your servants is found with it shall die, and we also will be my lord's servants." (vv. 3–9)

The steward pursued the brothers, stopped them on their journey, and asked, "Why have you repaid evil for good?" (v. 4). In other words, "Why have you stolen from Pharaoh's house, from the hand of Joseph, who has benefited you?" The brothers responded by saying that they had returned the money they found in their sacks from the first journey. Why would they be inclined to steal anything from Joseph?

Notice what they say: "Far be it from your servants to do such a thing!" (v. 7). It's very difficult for any human being to be falsely accused. Yet the brothers replied indignantly despite the fact that they had previously done things far worse than stealing Joseph's cup. They had stolen his whole life. They were more than capable of the kind of treachery they were accused of here. Then they added a singularly rash vow:

> "How then could we steal silver or gold from your lord's house? Whichever of your servants is found with it shall die, and we also will be my lord's servants." So the steward said, "Let it be as you say: he who is found with it shall be my servant, and the rest of you shall be innocent." (vv. 8–10)

At the last judgment, all people will be assembled in the divine tribunal and brought before God. The response of those who hear God's verdict on their sin will be silence. There won't be any protests. In other words, no one will stand before God and say, "Far be it from me to have done this or that." Jesus said that every idle word will be brought into judgment. Not just the idle words, but every word we've spoken and will speak will be placed before the scrutiny of almighty God. When God renders His verdict, every mouth will be stopped.

Our mouths will be stopped because it will be futile to argue with God. We know that His judgment will flow from His own omniscience, from His perfect knowledge of everything that we've ever done or thought or said.

> Then each man quickly lowered his sack to the ground, and each man opened his sack. And he searched, beginning with the eldest and ending with the youngest. And the cup was found in Benjamin's sack. Then they tore their clothes, and every man loaded his donkey, and they returned to the city. (vv. 11–13)

They couldn't wait to open their bags, for they were sure that they would be vindicated. That seems a little strange, given that they had already been surprised once before when they opened their sacks and found their money inside. You would think that by now they would have realized that something was going on and that they would be terrified to open their sacks.

In these Old Testament narratives, highly dramatic moments are often passed over briefly. Just one sentence says that they tore their clothes, loaded their donkeys, and started back to the city.

Try to imagine the pathos of this moment. As each additional sack is searched and is found not to contain Joseph's silver cup, they're beginning to feel more relieved, more comfortable, and more convinced that the charges against them are false. They get down to the very last sack, and of all places, there is Joseph's silver cup in Benjamin's sack. The Bible says, "They tore their clothes." That was an indication of the paroxysm of grief, terror, and mourning that came upon them.

> When Judah and his brothers came to Joseph's house, he was still there. They fell before him to the ground. Joseph said to them, "What deed is this that you have done? Do you not know that a man like me can indeed practice divination?" (vv. 14–15)

This was at least the third time that the dream Joseph had as a boy was fulfilled as they fell down before him. In speaking of practicing divination, Joseph was not saying that he was a magician. Rather, he was saying that as a man in his position he had insight and knowledge that were transcendent.

> And Judah said, "What shall we say to my lord? What shall we speak? Or how can we clear ourselves? God has found out the guilt of your servants; behold, we are my lord's servants, both we and he also in whose hand the cup has been found." (v. 16)

What did Judah have in mind when he said that? Was he persuaded that Benjamin had indeed stolen the cup? Was he accepting a part in his brother's guilt and asking Joseph to spread the blame around not just to Benjamin but to all of them? Or was something deeper going on?

Judah may have finally been recognizing the hand of God in all these events. He was realizing that even though he was not guilty of this particular crime, all this had befallen them because God knew the profound guilt they had been carrying around all these years.

But [Joseph] said: "Far be it from me that I should do so! Only the man in whose hand the cup was found shall be my servant. But as for you, go up in peace to your father." (v. 17)

Joseph essentially said: "I don't want you to be my slaves. You're innocent. I'm not going to punish the innocent with the guilty. I'm going to exact punishment only on the guilty one—Benjamin. He stays. He will be my slave. The rest of you can go back to your father." But Judah and the brothers would rather stay in Egypt as slaves than go back to Jacob without Benjamin. Going back without Benjamin was the worst thing that they could conceive of. Joseph was making them feel the weight of their dilemma with the full measure of intensity as they wondered, "What will happen next?"

# 16

# A Plea
# for the Guilty

In the previous chapter, we saw Judah ask Joseph to let all the brothers assume responsibility for the missing cup found in Benjamin's sack. Joseph rejected Judah's offer and said that the brothers could return home while Benjamin stayed in Egypt. Joseph's exact words were "Go up in peace to your father" (Gen. 44:17).

There's an underlying hint of irony in his statement. Joseph knew that there was no chance that his brothers could approach their father in peace in these circumstances. It would have been more accurate if Joseph had said, "Go home in anguish to your father." What follows is Judah's plea as he becomes the spokesman for the brothers as they try to intercede for Benjamin's safety.

> Then Judah went up to him and said, "Oh, my lord, please let your servant speak a word in my lord's ears, and let not your anger burn against your servant, for you are like Pharaoh himself. My lord asked his servants, saying, 'Have you a father, or a brother?' And we said to my lord, 'We have a father, an old man, and a young brother, the child of his old age. His brother is dead, and he alone is left of his mother's children, and his father loves him.' Then you said to your servants, 'Bring him down to me, that I may set my eyes on him.' We said to my lord, 'The boy cannot leave his father, for if he should leave his father, his father would die.' Then you said to your servants, 'Unless your youngest brother comes down with you, you shall not see my face again.'" (vv. 18–23)

Judah was pleading with Joseph. He was saying: "Don't you remember the conditions that you gave us for our return to Egypt? Now consider our fate. This isn't just about the younger brother that we've brought here. The father that you inquired about will surely die if we go home without our brother."

> "When we went back to your servant my father, we told him the words of my lord. And when our father said, 'Go again, buy us a little food,' we said, 'We cannot go down. If our youngest brother goes with us, then we will go down. For we cannot see the man's face unless our youngest brother is with us.' Then your servant my father said to us, 'You know that my wife bore me two sons. One left me, and I said, "Surely he has been torn to pieces," and I have never seen him since. If you take this one also from me, and harm happens to him, you will bring down my gray hairs in evil to Sheol.'" (vv. 24–29)

Judah tried to explain to Joseph the agony that their father had endured all those years. He thought he was pleading with a stranger. Yet no one in the world understood more clearly what Judah was talking about than Joseph. This is irony. As God brings His will to pass, His providence unfolds through the details, the subtle nuances, the twists and turns of seemingly minor events in history, and they become moments of importance in His hand.

Judah told Joseph that if he punished the boy, he was not just punishing Benjamin. He was saying, "I know that you don't want to punish the innocent with the guilty, but this will kill our father." He was pleading for mercy. "Think of this old man who loves his youngest son. His other son from his wife Rachel was torn from his hands." Judah didn't volunteer that this happened because of the brothers, but he reminded Joseph that the double calamity would be more than Jacob could bear.

> "Now therefore, as soon as I come to your servant my father, and the boy is not with us, then, as his life is bound up in the boy's life, as soon as he sees that the boy is not with us, he will die, and your servants will bring down the gray hairs of your servant our father with sorrow to Sheol. For your servant became a

pledge of safety for the boy to my father, saying, 'If I do not bring him back to you, then I shall bear the blame before my father all my life.' Now therefore, please let your servant remain instead of the boy as a servant to my lord, and let the boy go back with his brothers. For how can I go back to my father if the boy is not with me? I fear to see the evil that would find my father." (vv. 30–34)

This was an enormous plea for clemency. Judah was not asking Joseph to overlook the transgression. Rather, he was saying: "I had to beg my father to let this young one come with us. The only way he would part with him was on the condition that one of us would be a surety for him. I am the surety for my brother."

Judah proposed an act of vicarious punishment, an act of substitution: "Let me take his place. Let me act as the surety for my brother. Let him go for the sake of our father, and take me in his place. I will be your slave." Keep in mind that when Joseph's brothers had schemed to get rid of him, there were varying degrees of each brother's intentions and hostilities. Judah had proposed a less severe treatment of Joseph than the rest of the brothers sought.

Remember that among the sons of Jacob, the first-born, Reuben, did not receive the patriarchal blessing. The second son, Simeon, also did not receive the primogeniture, the patriarchal blessing of the inheritance, nor did the third-born, Levi. While Judah didn't receive the patriarchal blessing either, he was given the scepter.

When Jacob later blessed his sons, he said, "The scepter shall not depart from Judah, nor the ruler's staff from between his feet, until tribute comes to him; and to him shall be the obedience of the peoples" (49:10). Consequently, the kings of Israel, particularly those from the line of David, came from the tribe of Judah, to whom the kingdom was promised.

Judah's greater Son—greater than David—was Jesus, who became the King of kings. Jesus was from the tribe of Judah. One of the titles ascribed to Christ in the New Testament is "the Lion of the tribe of Judah" (Rev. 5:5). Here we find one of those moments in Old Testament history when a forebear of the Messiah typologically foreshadows the work of the Messiah. Judah offered himself as surety for his brother. In doing so, he promised to cover someone else's debts.

The supreme surety provided for the people of God came from the lineage of Judah. Jesus is our surety. Jesus is the One who takes on Himself the debts that we owe the King of the universe. Jesus is the One who stands in our place. Jesus is the One who substitutes Himself for us in bearing the just punishment of our sins. That's why when we speak of the atonement of Christ, we call it the vicarious or substitutionary atonement.

*Vicarious* describes something that is done for someone by someone else. Judah offered to submit to slavery so that Benjamin, who was perceived at this point to be guilty of the crime, would be set free. The New Testament is replete with this imagery with respect to the work of Christ, who comes to set the captives free. He binds Himself to the law and to the judgment of God so that He may set free those who have been held captive by their sin.

In this account of Judah, we see the gospel in a nutshell: the gospel of vicarious sacrifice, the gospel of vicarious punishment. That's the offer that Judah made to the prime minister of Egypt—to suffer on Benjamin's behalf—when he kept his vow to be a surety for his brother.

# 17

# The Revelation

Judah's impassioned plea on Benjamin's behalf must be one of the most eloquent pleas for mercy ever recorded. In legal dramas in movies and on television, we see dramatic responses to the attorneys' pleas and arguments, but life rarely resembles those fictional scenarios. Here, however, there is a dramatic response from Joseph to Judah's promise to be a surety for Benjamin.

"Then Joseph could not control himself before all those who stood by him. He cried, 'Make everyone go out from me'" (Gen. 45:1). As we have seen, Joseph had been trying to lead his brothers to a deeper awareness of the seriousness of their sin. We saw all his machinations, including the hiding of money in the brothers' sacks as well as the hiding of Joseph's silver cup in Benjamin's sack.

Through all of this, Joseph had been pretending. He had been feigning righteous indignation against his brothers' alleged theft. Sometimes it's hard for a person to carry on a charade without breaking. Joseph had finally reached the end of his self-restraint. Upon hearing Judah's offer to be a surety for Benjamin, Joseph was so deeply moved that he could no longer contain himself. Judah brought the saga to an end by his heroic offer to be a substitute for his brother.

> So no one stayed with him when Joseph made himself known to his brothers. And he wept aloud, so that the Egyptians heard it, and the household of Pharaoh heard it. And Joseph said to his brothers, "I am Joseph!" (vv. 1–3)

With Joseph's authority as prime minister, his staff obeyed him instantly and left his presence, leaving him alone with his brothers. Joseph broke down, weeping and wailing so loudly that the Egyptians who had departed from his presence heard him crying.

Joseph's revealing himself is one of the most dramatic moments in this whole episode and certainly one of the most dramatic moments that Joseph's brothers ever experienced in their lives. In all his previous meetings with the brothers, Joseph had communicated with them through an interpreter. Joseph's Egyptian name was Zaphenath-paneah, but Joseph didn't say that name to his brothers. Instead, speaking in his native tongue, he revealed himself by his Hebrew name: "I am Joseph!"

Just think of the emotions that were boiling inside the brothers. They were already terrified, having been caught with the hidden cup. They had just listened to Judah's plea to let him be a substitute for Benjamin, and they didn't know how the situation would be resolved. Now as they were standing in the presence of the prime minister—who was dressed in Egyptian clothing, who bore Egyptian symbols of authority, and who had been speaking in the Egyptian language all this time—he suddenly spoke to them in Hebrew and seemed to claim to be their long-lost brother.

> "I am Joseph! Is my father still alive?" But his brothers could not answer him, for they were dismayed at his presence. So Joseph said to his brothers, "Come near to me, please." And they came near. (vv. 3–4)

This was a stunning shock. Joseph? *The* Joseph? Our brother Joseph? They couldn't even answer. They were stunned and speechless before him. He didn't command them to come; he invited them to come. Perhaps something in Joseph's tone of voice assured them that it was safe, and they approached him.

> And he said, "I am your brother, Joseph, whom you sold into Egypt. And now do not be distressed or angry with yourselves because you sold me here, for God sent me before you to preserve life. For the famine has been in the land these two years, and there are yet five years in which there

will be neither plowing nor harvest. And God sent me before you to preserve for you a remnant on earth, and to keep alive for you many survivors. So it was not you who sent me here, but God. He has made me a father to Pharaoh, and lord of all his house and ruler over all the land of Egypt." (vv. 4–8)

Joseph told his brothers that God had sent him to Egypt to save their lives. Years earlier, they had ruthlessly sought to take his life and ended up selling his life for a few pieces of silver. But in the providence of God, Joseph had been placed in Egypt for this moment in history to provide their physical salvation.

"Hurry and go up to my father and say to him, 'Thus says your son Joseph, God has made me lord of all Egypt. Come down to me; do not tarry. You shall dwell in the land of Goshen, and you shall be near me, you and your children and your children's children, and your flocks, your herds, and all that you have. There I will provide for you, for there are yet five years of famine to come, so that you and your household, and all that you have, do not come to poverty.' And now your eyes see, and the eyes of my brother Benjamin see, that it is my mouth that speaks to you. You must tell my father of all my honor in Egypt, and of all that you have seen. Hurry and bring my father down here." Then he fell upon his brother Benjamin's neck and wept, and Benjamin wept upon his neck. And he kissed all his brothers and wept upon them. After that his brothers talked with him.

When the report was heard in Pharaoh's house, "Joseph's brothers have come," it pleased Pharaoh and his servants. (vv. 9–16)

This is a touching scene. Joseph first kissed Benjamin, and he wept. Then he kissed each of his other brothers, and they spoke to one another.

Everyone in the palace must have been talking and wondering what was going on. They'd heard the prime minister weeping. They were fearing the worst, but then they found out it was good news. He was crying for joy. The prime minister's brothers had come.

We can only assume that at some point, the story of Joseph's past had been relayed to Pharaoh and his staff. They all knew that Joseph had come from prison. So when he was brought from prison to Pharaoh's court and exalted over the rest of the administrators in the land, everyone was asking about his background and pedigree. They knew that he was a Hebrew, so how had he come to be in Potiphar's house in the first place?

It seems likely that those who were intimately associated with Joseph had some idea of his estrangement from his brothers. Now they were buzzing with the news that Joseph's brothers had arrived. It pleased Pharaoh and his servants. It is beautiful to witness genuine reconciliation between estranged parties—not just a guarded truce, but real reconciliation. We take delight when love triumphs over hatred.

And Pharaoh said to Joseph, "Say to your brothers, 'Do this: load your beasts and go back to the land of Canaan, and take your father and your households, and come to me, and I will give you the best of the land of Egypt, and you shall eat the fat of the land.' And you, Joseph, are commanded to say, 'Do this: take wagons from the land of Egypt for your little ones and for your wives, and bring your father, and come. Have no concern for your goods, for the best of all the land of Egypt is yours.'" (vv. 17–20)

Pharaoh said to Joseph in effect: "I'm not giving an invitation; this is a command. Bring the whole family—not just your father, but all the children, grandchildren, and livestock—and don't tell me that there's not enough land for you. I'm giving you the best parcel of land in all Egypt. I'm giving you the land of Goshen. Don't tell me that the journey is too arduous and that you can't bring the things that are precious to you. Take all the carts you need to transport everything that you want down here." This is an incredible offer by Pharaoh.

The sons of Israel did so: and Joseph gave them wagons, according to the command of Pharaoh, and gave them provisions for the journey. To each and all of them he gave a change of clothes, but to

Benjamin he gave three hundred shekels of silver and five changes of clothes. To his father he sent as follows: ten donkeys loaded with the good things of Egypt, and ten female donkeys loaded with grain, bread, and provision for his father on the journey. Then he sent his brothers away, and as they departed, he said to them, "Do not quarrel on the way." (vv. 21–24)

In telling them not to quarrel, Joseph was saying: "We've just made peace. We've just experienced reconciliation. I can't wait to see my father and the rest of the family. Let's maintain decorum." This shows Joseph's wisdom. Can you imagine these brothers walking out of there, in stunned disbelief? They were going home, and they had good news to tell Jacob. They couldn't wait to say, "Your son is alive; he is the prime minister!" Yet they were also afraid of Jacob's response. "What do you mean, he's alive? How did he get to Egypt? I thought you said that he was killed by an animal."

Truth was going to come out when the brothers returned to Jacob, and Joseph was thinking that the brothers were liable to kill one another on the way home. They could start arguing, "I told you not to do that" or "This was all your idea," and they could destroy one another before they ever got back home to tell Jacob the good news.

> So they went up out of Egypt and came to the land of Canaan to their father Jacob. And they told him, "Joseph is still alive, and he is ruler over all the land of Egypt." And his heart became numb, for he did not believe them. (vv. 25–26)

How could his heart have done anything else? He was afraid to believe it. He couldn't take it in. Jacob had to wrestle with his own faith in God about the news he had just heard.

# 18

# It Is Enough

After executing an extended ruse to bring his brothers to repentance, Joseph finally revealed his true identity to them. He then sent them home to gather the entire family and bring them back to Egypt. Joseph gave them provisions for their journey and bestowed enormous wealth on his full brother, Benjamin. When the brothers returned home and told Jacob that Joseph was still alive, Jacob's "heart became numb" (Gen. 45:26). He was reluctant to believe the report of his sons.

But when they told him all the words of Joseph, which he had said to them, and when he saw the wagons that Joseph had sent to carry him, the spirit of their father Jacob revived. And Israel said, "It is enough; Joseph my son is still alive. I will go and see him before I die." (vv. 27–28)

Jacob's statement here reminds us of a biblical character in the New Testament who said something similar: the righteous and devout Simeon. Simeon had waited many years for the fulfillment of the promise that the Holy Spirit had made to him: that he would not die until he saw the Lord's Messiah.

When Joseph and Mary brought the infant Jesus to the temple, Simeon saw Him, picked Him up in his arms, and sang the Nunc Dimittis:

"Lord, now you are letting your servant depart in
        peace,
    according to your word;
for my eyes have seen your salvation

that you have prepared in the presence of all
peoples,
a light for revelation to the Gentiles,
and for glory to your people Israel."
(Luke 2:29–32)

That's what Jacob said in his advanced age: "It is enough. Now I can depart." In troubling times, we can easily say: "That's enough. I don't want any more." In happy times, however, do we ever say that it's enough? When do we ever reach that place in the journey of life of being truly content and satisfied? As we age, we tend to adjust our goals. We don't have a lot of aspirations left because we don't have a lot of time left to reach them. Even then, we still hope that something will come into our lives that will fully satisfy all the longings of our hearts. But rarely do we say, "It is enough." Yet Jacob did say it, for he had received the greatest news that he could ever receive. His son who was dead was alive.

This reminds me of the father in the parable of the prodigal son. When he saw his younger son coming home, nothing could exceed his joy in that moment. That's why the father held a big celebration that provoked the envy of the older brother. But the father responded: "Don't you see? My son was dead and now is alive. He's gone and he's now returned" (see Luke 15:11–32). Similarly, Jacob was saying, "Let me see Joseph once, and then I can die in peace a happy man."

The story continues in Genesis 46:

> So Israel took his journey with all that he had and came to Beersheba, and offered sacrifices to the God of his father Isaac. And God spoke to Israel in visions of the night and said, "Jacob, Jacob." (vv. 1–2)

Jacob was thrilled beyond words to hear the good news about Joseph. He set off and got as far as Beersheba, and then he offered a sacrifice to God. If we read between the lines, we might suspect that Jacob was beginning to get nervous as he approached the border. After all, he'd been the victim of his sons' lies before. So he offered a sacrifice to God and prayed.

Jacob was not a paper saint; he was a human being. There were probably many moments in his life when he felt the absence of God rather than the presence of God, when the fears of the flesh took hold of him. Not very long before this, Jacob had said: "Joseph is no more, and Simeon is no more. . . . All this has come against me" (42:36). Jacob had come close to falling into the pit of despair. So now God appeared again at night in a dream—as He had done with Abraham and as He had done earlier with Jacob—and He spoke to Jacob in this dream.

Notice that God does not say to him, "Jacob," but He repeats his name and says, "Jacob, Jacob" (46:2). There are several occasions in Scripture when someone is addressed in this manner. On Mount Moriah, Abraham was poised to sacrifice his son Isaac when at the last second, God called to him, saying: "Abraham, Abraham! . . . Do not lay your hand on the boy" (22:11–12).

God called the young Samuel in a midnight vision, saying: "'Samuel! Samuel!' And Samuel said, 'Speak, for your servant hears'" (1 Sam. 3:10). When David received news of the death of his son, he cried out in agony, "O my son Absalom, my son, my son Absalom!" (2 Sam. 18:33). As Elisha saw Elijah going up to heaven in a whirlwind, he cried out: "My father, my father! The chariots of Israel and its horsemen!" (2 Kings 2:12).

We see this type of address in the New Testament as well. Jesus spoke tenderly to Martha, saying, "Martha, Martha" (Luke 10:41). In His lament over Jerusalem, Jesus said: "O Jerusalem, Jerusalem, the city that kills the prophets and stones those who are sent to it! How often would I have gathered your children together as a hen gathers her brood under her wings, and you were not willing!" (Matt. 23:37). When Peter boldly presumed that he would never betray Jesus, Jesus looked at him and declared, "Simon, Simon, behold, Satan demanded to have you, that he might sift you like wheat, but I have prayed for you that your faith may not fail" (Luke 22:31–32). Saul, while on the road to Damascus, saw the bright light at midday and heard a voice in the Hebrew tongue calling to him, "Saul, Saul, why are you persecuting me?" (Acts 9:4).

Perhaps the most poignant use of name repetition occurred on the cross when Jesus cried, "'Eli, Eli, lema sabachthani?' that is, 'My God, my God, why have you forsaken me?'" (Matt. 27:46). This repetition of the personal form of address in Scripture is a Hebrew device that signifies deep personal intimacy. Jesus used this device in the Sermon on the Mount: on the last day, many will say to Him, "Lord, Lord"—pretending not only to know Him but to be His close personal friend, to be on an intimate basis with Him—but He will respond, "I never knew you; depart from me" (Matt. 7:22–23).

In the midst of Jacob's uncertainty and fear, God spoke to him with this same intimate repetition.

"Jacob, Jacob." And [ Jacob] said, "Here I am." Then he said, "I am God, the God of your father. Do not be afraid to go down to Egypt, for there I will make you into a great nation. I myself will go down with you to Egypt, and I will also bring you up again, and Joseph's hand shall close your eyes." (Gen. 46:2–4)

God renewed His covenant promise; He renewed the pledge that He had given years earlier to Jacob to be with him in his sojourn.

> Then Jacob set out from Beersheba. The sons of Israel carried Jacob their father, their little ones, and their wives, in the wagons that Pharaoh had sent to carry him. They also took their livestock and their goods, which they had gained in the land of Canaan, and came into Egypt, Jacob and all his offspring with him, his sons, and his sons' sons with him, his daughters, and his sons' daughters. All his offspring he brought with him into Egypt. (vv. 5–7)

What follows in the rest of chapter 46 is a lengthy list of all the people who went with Jacob. The narrative picks up again in verse 26:

> All the persons belonging to Jacob who came into Egypt, who were his own descendants, not including Jacob's sons' wives, were sixty-six persons in all. And

the sons of Joseph, who were born to him in Egypt, were two. All the persons of the house of Jacob who came into Egypt were seventy.

He had sent Judah ahead of him to Joseph to show the way before him in Goshen, and they came into the land of Goshen. Then Joseph prepared his chariot and went up to meet Israel his father in Goshen. He presented himself to him and fell on his neck and wept on his neck a good while. (vv. 26–29)

This is an interesting description of Jacob and Joseph's reunion. It wasn't just an emotional hug, a kiss on the cheek, and a warm embrace. Joseph fell on his father's neck and wept, and he just hung on. What do you say after all those years?

Israel said to Joseph, "Now let me die, since I have seen your face and know that you are still alive." (v. 30)

After all the years in prison, after all the time in exile, after all the loneliness in Joseph's life, his greatest dream was fulfilled. After a similar period of mourning and grief in Jacob's soul, his deepest dream was fulfilled. The father saw his son, and the son saw his father. It was enough. It was enough for Joseph, and it was enough for Jacob.

# 19

# Pharaoh's Steward

We've seen all along that Joseph was supremely gifted by God, particularly in the realm of administration. That emerged early when he was placed over Potiphar's household, as well as later in prison when the warden put Joseph in charge. Joseph's gifting eventually led to Pharaoh's appointing of Joseph as prime minister of Egypt.

We gain even more insights into Joseph's extraordinary gifts in Genesis 47:

Now there was no food in all the land, for the famine was very severe, so that the land of Egypt and the land of Canaan languished by reason of the famine. And Joseph gathered up all the money that was found in the land of Egypt and in the land of Canaan, in exchange for the grain that they bought. And Joseph brought the money into Pharaoh's house. And when the money was all spent in the land of Egypt and in the land of Canaan, all the Egyptians came to Joseph and said, "Give us food. Why should we die before your eyes? For our money is gone." (vv. 13–15)

The people had purchased from the government the grain they needed to relieve their starvation. Of course, money is valuable only as a means of exchange. You can't eat it; you can't wear it; you can't build homes out of it. Eventually, the people ran out of money and came to Joseph for food. "And Joseph answered, 'Give your livestock, and I will give you food in exchange for your livestock, if your money is gone.' So they brought their livestock to Joseph, and

Joseph gave them food in exchange for the horses, the flocks, the herds, and the donkeys. He supplied them with food in exchange for all their livestock that year" (vv. 16–17).

Some might look at this program and see Joseph as a ruthless tyrant. The people were starving, but there was still grain in Egypt's storehouses. Instead of just giving grain to the people, Joseph first sold it to them. Then, when their money was gone, he instituted a bartering system, allowing them to purchase grain by trading their livestock. The question is, Should Joseph have simply given the food to the people?

We must remember that Joseph was responsible for stewarding the entire nation's resources, and the people did have means by which they could purchase grain. They just purchased it using a barter system rather than with hard currency. This shows Joseph's fiscal responsibility. If the people had absolutely nothing, then perhaps Joseph would have given them the grain. As long as they could pay something in exchange for the goods they were receiving, however, he required it from them. This is an example of his prudence in management.

And when that year was ended, they came to him the following year and said to him, "We will not hide from my lord that our money is all spent. The herds of livestock are my lord's. There is nothing left in the sight of my lord but our bodies and our land. Why should we die before your eyes, both we and our land? Buy us and our land for food, and we with our land will be servants to Pharaoh. And give us seed that we may live and not die, and that the land may not be desolate."

So Joseph bought all the land of Egypt for Pharaoh, for all the Egyptians sold their fields, because the famine was severe on them. The land became Pharaoh's. As for the people, he made servants of them from one end of Egypt to the other. Only the land of the priests he did not buy, for the priests had a fixed allowance from Pharaoh and lived on the allowance that Pharaoh gave them; therefore they did not sell their land.

Then Joseph said to the people, "Behold, I have this day bought you and your land for Pharaoh. Now here is seed for you, and you shall sow the land. And at the harvests you shall give a fifth to Pharaoh, and four fifths shall be your own, as seed for the field and as food for yourselves and your households, and as food for your little ones." And they said, "You have saved our lives; may it please my lord, we will be servants to Pharaoh." So Joseph made it a statute concerning the land of Egypt, and it stands to this day, that Pharaoh should have the fifth; the land of the priests alone did not become Pharaoh's. (vv. 18–26)

The people had run out of money to purchase grain and livestock to barter for grain, but they still had two things left. First, they had their land, which was now desolate and worthless because it had already been harvested. Second, they had their freedom. They told Joseph that they were willing to enter indentured servitude if he would feed them. A free transaction was still taking place between Joseph and the people.

Joseph wasn't confiscating the land. He was purchasing the land by barter. He was exchanging the food for ownership of the property. The Egyptian farmers could still farm the land; they paid 20 percent of what they produced to Egypt, and the other 80 percent was theirs. This was a system of managing the economy by which there was a partnership between the nation and the individual farmer that was entered into freely.

Of course, such an arrangement can devolve into an exploitive system when unscrupulous rulers and governors then increase that tax, increase the demands on the people, and bleed their resources dry. Here, however, we see Joseph acting in a humanitarian way. He preserved the lives of his people, he preserved the dignity of his people, and he preserved the production of the land for future generations.

As the conclusion to the narrative of Joseph's life draws near, we are told in chapter 48 that Jacob became ill and was approaching the end of his life. Joseph came to see his father, seeking Jacob's blessing on Joseph's two sons, Ephraim and Manasseh.

> And Israel stretched out his right hand and laid it on the head of Ephraim, who was the younger, and his left hand on the head of Manasseh, crossing his hands (for Manasseh was the firstborn). . . . When Joseph saw that his father laid his right hand on the

head of Ephraim, it displeased him, and he took his father's hand to move it from Ephraim's head to Manasseh's head. And Joseph said to his father, "Not this way, my father; since this one is the first-born, put your right hand on his head." But his father refused and said, "I know, my son, I know. He also shall become a people, and he also shall be great. Nevertheless, his younger brother shall be greater than he, and his offspring shall become a multitude of nations." (vv. 14, 17–19)

As the firstborn, Manasseh would traditionally have received the birthright. When Jacob went to bless the children, however, he reversed the order. He placed his right hand on Ephraim and his left hand on Manasseh. Joseph objected that Jacob was blessing the second-born rather than the firstborn. Yet Jacob persisted. In the same way that Jacob had received the blessing from his father—even though Jacob was not the firstborn—so God, to show the sovereignty of His electing grace in this human incident, again broke the tradition and blessed the younger rather than the elder.

# 20

# Take Me Back
# to Canaan

Joseph had reunited with his father and his brothers, and he brought the entire family from Canaan to the land of Goshen in Egypt. Jacob approached death, and Genesis 49 recounts the patriarchal blessing that he gave to his sons. This blessing served as a kind of prophetic instrument to the future of the nation of Israel. After Jacob blessed his sons, we read:

> Then he commanded them and said to them, "I am to be gathered to my people; bury me with my fathers in the cave that is in the field of Ephron the

Hittite, in the cave that is in the field at Machpelah, to the east of Mamre, in the land of Canaan, which Abraham bought with the field from Ephron the Hittite to possess as a burying place. There they buried Abraham and Sarah his wife. There they buried Isaac and Rebekah his wife, and there I buried Leah—the field and the cave that is in it were bought from the Hittites." When Jacob finished commanding his sons, he drew up his feet into the bed and breathed his last and was gathered to his people. (vv. 29–33)

This was a poignant moment for Joseph—the death of his beloved father, Jacob—and Jacob's final instructions were for his resting place. He wanted to be buried with his fathers in Machpelah, which reminds us of one of the great ironies of the patriarchal history. We remember that this whole drama began when God called Abram, already an old man at that point, out of Ur of the Chaldeans. God promised that Abram would be the father of a great nation and that his descendants would be as numerous as the stars of the sky and the sand of the sea.

Integral to that promise of the great inheritance was the promise of land, which then became the promised land. Yet we are told in the New Testament that Abraham "went out, not knowing where he was going" (Heb. 11:8). Hoping against hope, he trusted God for his future and became the father of the faithful (Rom. 4:18). The irony was this: the only piece of real estate that Abraham ever owned in the promised land was Machpelah, his cemetery plot. That was his personal inheritance in the promised land.

Machpelah became more or less a family shrine. Abraham and Sarah were buried there. Isaac and Rebekah were buried there. Jacob's first wife, Leah, was buried there. As he was dying, Jacob asked that he might also be buried there, that he might enter his rest in the presence of the One who would be known in future generations as the God of Abraham, Isaac, and Jacob. Then Jacob died.

> Then Joseph fell on his father's face and wept over him and kissed him. And Joseph commanded his servants the physicians to embalm his father. So

the physicians embalmed Israel. Forty days were
required for it, for that is how many are required
for embalming. And the Egyptians wept for him
seventy days. (50:1–3)

It may sound a little macabre that when Jacob died,
Joseph kissed him. People in our day are often squea-
mish about kissing corpses because something happens
instantly upon death. The outward appearance of a dead
person becomes strange and frightening when life has
left the body. It's even worse after rigor mortis has set in.

Yet in kissing Jacob, Joseph gave a last outward
expression of affection for his father. This is a very nat-
ural reaction to the passing of a loved one and a custom
that has persisted for thousands of years. It is not something extraordinary or strange.

And when the days of weeping for him were past,
Joseph spoke to the household of Pharaoh, saying,
"If now I have found favor in your eyes, please speak
in the ears of Pharaoh, saying, 'My father made me
swear, saying, "I am about to die: in my tomb that

I have hewed out for myself in the land of Canaan, there shall you bury me." Now therefore, let me please go up and bury my father. Then I will return."

And Pharaoh answered, "Go up, and bury your father, as he made you swear." So Joseph went up to bury his father. With him went up all the servants of Pharaoh, the elders of his household, and all the elders of the land of Egypt, as well as all the household of Joseph, his brothers, and his father's household. Only their children, their flocks, and their herds were left in the land of Goshen. And there went up with him both chariots and horsemen. It was a very great company. (vv. 4–9)

Joseph asked for a leave of absence from his duties as prime minister to go and bury his father. Jacob's funeral procession was a massive affair; Joseph's family, members of Pharaoh's court, and Joseph's servants participated in this journey for Jacob's funeral.

When they came to the threshing floor of Atad, which is beyond the Jordan, they lamented there with a very great and grievous lamentation, and he made a mourning for his father seven days. When the inhabitants of the land, the Canaanites, saw the mourning on the threshing floor of Atad, they said, "This is a grievous mourning by the Egyptians." Therefore the place was named Abel-mizraim; it is beyond the Jordan. Thus his sons did for him as he had commanded them, for his sons carried him to the land of Canaan and buried him in the cave of the field at Machpelah, to the east of Mamre, which Abraham bought with the field from Ephron the Hittite to possess as a burying place. After he had buried his father, Joseph returned to Egypt with his brothers and all who had gone up with him to bury his father. (vv. 10–14)

Now that Jacob had died, a new sense of terror entered the hearts of Joseph's brothers. They realized that Joseph had been kind to them and had refrained from vengeance out of his love for his father. Now that their father was gone, in a real sense, the brothers of

Joseph were experiencing the loss of their protector. They were thinking among themselves, "Now what is Joseph going to do?"

> When Joseph's brothers saw that their father was dead, they said, "It may be that Joseph will hate us and pay us back for all the evil that we did to him." So they sent a message to Joseph, saying, "Your father gave this command before he died: 'Say to Joseph, "Please forgive the transgression of your brothers and their sin, because they did evil to you."' And now, please forgive the transgression of the servants of the God of your father." Joseph wept when they spoke to him. His brothers also came and fell down before him and said, "Behold, we are your servants." (vv. 15–18)

Joseph's brothers still were not dealing directly with the problem of their guilt before him. They didn't send a letter to Joseph, saying: "We confess to you that we have done this evil against you. Please forgive us." Rather, they couched their confession in this indirect reference to Jacob. They were still appealing to Jacob as their protector.

As the brothers bowed down again before Joseph, we see another literal fulfillment of the original dream that created all this hostility in the first place. The teenage Joseph had dreamed of sheaves of wheat bowing down before him, meaning that at some point his brothers would bow before him. When he told his brothers his dreams, they were enraged and filled with jealousy and hatred. That's what had precipitated their betrayal of Joseph in the first place, and now the fulfillment of the dream seems like a broken record. This is the fourth or fifth time that they bowed down before him and offered themselves as slaves to Joseph's household.

But Joseph said to them, "Do not fear, for am I in the place of God? As for you, you meant evil against me, but God meant it for good, to bring it about that many people should be kept alive, as they are today. So do not fear; I will provide for you and your little ones." Thus he comforted them and spoke kindly to them. (vv. 19–21)

This text is crucial to the classical doctrine of divine providence, specifically as it relates to a subcategory of providence called concurrence. The doctrine of concurrence points to the mysterious way that God governs the affairs of human beings whereby even though we act according to our own desires, choices, and wills, God brings His sovereign will to pass not apart from the choices and actions of people but in, through, and by the work of people. Two streams are flowing—the human stream and the divine stream—but these two merge into one.

That's what Joseph was saying to his brothers when he observed, "You meant evil against me, but God meant it for good." He put his accent on the intent of the action. He was saying that when his brothers betrayed him, they weren't the only actors in the drama. God was involved, and God was working His good plan even through their evil plan. That's hard for us to grasp, but it's a principle that we find throughout Scripture.

God worked through Pharaoh to bring about His redemptive work of the exodus. Pharaoh meant it for evil; God meant it for good. God worked through the betrayal of Judas to accomplish the atonement of Christ. Judas meant it for evil, and he's responsible for his wicked intention. Yet God's intent was perfectly righteous. We see in this enormously important passage a reaffirmation that God is Lord of history. Joseph was saying that even though what the brothers did was evil, God was bringing everything together for good for those who love Him (see Rom. 8:28). God worked through their treachery to provide for their own salvation, their own rescue from famine. God used their evil intents for His righteous purposes.

> So Joseph remained in Egypt, he and his father's house. Joseph lived 110 years. And Joseph saw Ephraim's children of the third generation. The children also of Machir the son of Manasseh were counted as Joseph's own. And Joseph said to his brothers, "I am about to die, but God will visit you and bring you up out of this land to the land that he swore to Abraham, to Isaac, and to Jacob." Then Joseph made the sons of Israel swear, saying, "God will surely visit you, and you shall carry up

my bones from here." So Joseph died, being 110 years old. They embalmed him, and he was put in a coffin in Egypt. (Gen. 50:22–26)

Joseph's last words regarding the future work of God were prophetic. God, at a later date, would once again be present among His people and would remove them from Egypt and take them to the promised land. Though the story of Joseph's life ends as the book of Genesis concludes, it's not quite the end of what the Bible says about this man. The book of Exodus begins with this ominous statement: "Now there arose a new king over Egypt, who did not know Joseph" (Ex. 1:8).

What follows is the story of what took place four hundred years after Jacob's family moved to the land of Goshen. There arose a new king who didn't know Joseph, who had forgotten Joseph. He wasn't concerned to honor the pledge that Joseph had made to his family and the pledge that the earlier pharaoh had made to protect these people. The new pharaoh enslaved the Israelites, setting the stage for the most dramatic act of redemption in the whole Old Testament: the exodus of Israel out of Egypt. The Bible tells us later in Exodus that before Moses led the Israelites into the wilderness, he took Joseph's bones with him to fulfill the promise that had been made (Ex. 13:19).

As we complete this study of Joseph, may we not be like Pharaoh, who forgot Joseph, but may we remember this story from sacred Scripture and marvel at the wonder of God's sovereignty, drawing strength and encouragement despite all the ups and downs of our own lives, trusting that the same God who orchestrated the events of Joseph's life for good has not changed and that He is working good for those who love Him and are called according to His purpose (Rom. 8:28).

# About the Author

Dr. R.C. Sproul was founder of Ligonier Ministries, first minister of preaching and teaching at Saint Andrew's Chapel in Sanford, Fla., first president of Reformation Bible College, and executive editor of *Tabletalk* magazine. His radio program, *Renewing Your Mind*, is still broadcast daily on hundreds of radio stations around the world and can also be heard online. He was author of more than one hundred books, including *The Holiness of God*, *Chosen by God*, and *Everyone's a Theologian*. He was recognized throughout the world for his articulate defense of the inerrancy of Scripture and the need for God's people to stand with conviction upon His Word.